MICAH
Who Is Like God?

Richard Caldwell

KRESS
BIBLICAL
RESOURCES

Published by:
Kress Biblical Resources
www.kressbiblical.com

ISBN: 978-1-934952-37-5

DEDICATION

To

My father and mother. I am blessed to have been loved and cared for by such people. My memories are good ones and that is because you both were good to us, by the grace of God.

Contents

ACKNOWLEDGMENTS

I am grateful for the tireless editing efforts of Jim and Gail Swindle — faithful servants, and faithful friends. I am blessed, and I give God thanks for you both.

1
GOD'S UNLIKELY MEANS
(1:1-8)

The true God is not to be trifled with—ever. He is often patient with sin because of His love for sinners, but He never ignores it. He may seem tame and distant because He has not yet judged your sin—giving you space for repentance—but be certain, when He decides to act against sin, His presence is dreadful.

He is the God who acts in the present, but His perspective and purposes are never confined to the present. He has declared the end from the beginning. Therefore, He can deal with men in a way that both reproves them and reassures them. He can reprove present disobedience, and reassure as to an ultimate end, because of His never-ending faithfulness.

He accomplishes His work among men in surprising ways. He confounds the wise, using means that men consider foolish. He confounds the strong, using means that men consider weak. He confounds conventional thinking and common assumptions, working in ways that men never expect.

We see all of this in the book of Micah.

This book bears the name of the man whom the Lord sent from the hamlet of Moresheth-Gath to the city of Jerusalem, and through whom the Lord spoke to both the northern and southern kingdoms, the cities of Samaria and Jerusalem.

The first verse gives us a glimpse into what will unfold before us in the next seven chapters. It gives us an opportunity to think about the mission, the man, the moment, and the message.

THE MISSION (1:1a)

The mission is described in the opening words of the book. *The Word of Yahweh that came to Micah.* That Word imparted a mission.

A mission from God is always the result of sovereign grace. God's prophets are the result of His saving work. Micah is a redeemed man who speaks for the God who had mercy upon him. Micah is to declare both God's wrath and God's mercy. Strange as it may seem, the declaration of God's approaching wrath is an act of mercy. God could have brought judgment without warning, but he didn't. He sent His Word—this burden—to his servant Micah. It was to be both proclaimed and written. HIS MISSION: TO COMMUNICATE THE WORD OF GOD.

That is also our mission. Though we no longer see prophets like Micah, the mission imparted by the gift of God's revelation still stands. God has deposited His Word into our care as a stewardship. We are bound by that stewardship to declare the Word of God faithfully. We dwell amid a people on their way to judgment. God does not owe warnings nor opportunities for salvation, but He has sent us forth with the message of His wrath and the gospel of forgiveness. We need to see ourselves as messengers of God, because that is what we are. God's plan for getting His Word to the world is us, the church. It's you. It's me.

THE MAN (1:1b)

God gave this mission to an unlikely man. His name, Micah, is a shortened version of the name Micaiah, which means "Who is like Yahweh?"

Micah is faithful to the meaning of his name. He declares that truth, that there is no one like God. In fact, he closes this book with that very declaration (7:18-20). God, through Micah, is pointing forward to all that He was going to accomplish through the One Who was to come, the Messiah. In this age, we are looking back on what God has already accomplished—the way of complete forgiveness, treading our iniquities underfoot through Jesus.

Micah apparently does not come from a stately family. People were often introduced as the son of their father, as was the case with Isaiah. Micah's father's name is not given. Rather, he is identified by the little village from which he came, Moresheth. It was about 25 miles southwest of Jerusalem.

Moresheth was such an insignificant place that it had to be identified by something larger than itself. It is called Moresheth-Gath (1:14), that is, Moresheth in the region of Gath. Gath was a major Philistine city, and this was a little community that bordered Philistia.

The only thing we know about this prophet, outside of what we have here, comes from the mention of him in Jeremiah 26:18. But the reference in Jeremiah is a powerful one. It tells us that Micah was remembered 100 years after his preaching ministry was over. At that time, God used the memory of this prophet to save the life of another—Jeremiah. See Jeremiah 26:12-19.

Micah was one of God's unlikely means. He was more familiar with common rural people in the lowlands than with the city of Jerusalem and the power brokers who lived there. God sent him from a powerless village to preach to the power centers of his day on behalf of the Creator of the Universe.

Question: Are you thoroughly convinced that ministry is the work of God? Are you convinced that God, though making use of men, is never limited by the powers of men? Are you so convinced of this that you are no longer impressed and impressionable when it comes to what this world fawns over, and you look to God to work in you and to use you?

1 Corinthians 1:26–31 *For consider your calling, brothers: not many of you were wise according to worldly standards, not many were powerful, not many were of noble birth. [27] But God chose what is foolish in the world to shame the wise; God chose what is weak in the world to shame the strong; [28] God chose what is low and despised in the world, even things that are not, to bring to nothing things that are, [29] so that no human being might boast in the presence of God. [30] And because of him you are in Christ Jesus, who became to us wisdom from God, righteousness and sanctification and redemption, [31] so that, as it is written, "Let the one who boasts, boast in the Lord."*

THE MOMENT (1:1c)

Every man's story is in some way a product of his times. Micah was prepared by God for the time in which he would serve. He served during the entire reign of wicked king Ahaz. On each side of those terrible 16 years, he preached during the reigns of two other kings of Judah. Before Ahaz was Jotham, and after Ahaz was Hezekiah. We don't know how long he preached before Ahaz, or how long he preached during the reign of Hezekiah. His ministry lasted somewhere between 20 and 50 years.

May I encourage you? During the reign of Ahaz, no one would have foreseen the revival that would come under Hezekiah.

Jotham was a good king, but there was still idolatry in the land under his reign. But **Ahaz was an exceedingly wicked king.** Apart from God's sustaining grace, the level of darkness under wicked Ahaz would have seemed completely hopeless. There were great abominations. Ahaz seemed to envy the idolatry that was characterizing the northern kingdom and the surrounding nations. He burned his own sons to death as offerings to false gods (2 Chron 28:3). The verses are haunting.

2 Chronicles 28:23 *In the time of his distress he became yet more faithless to the LORD-- this same King Ahaz.* ²³ *For he sacrificed to the gods of Damascus that had defeated him and said, "Because the gods of the kings of Syria helped them, I will sacrifice to them that they may help me." But they were the ruin of him and of all Israel.* ²⁴ *And Ahaz gathered together the vessels of the house of God and cut in pieces the vessels of the house of God, and he shut up the doors of the house of the LORD, and he made himself altars in every corner of Jerusalem.* ²⁵ *In every city of Judah he made high places to make offerings to other gods, provoking to anger the LORD, the God of his fathers.* ²⁶ *Now the rest of his acts and all his ways, from first to last, behold, they are written in the Book of the Kings of Judah and Israel.* ²⁷ *And Ahaz slept with his fathers, and they buried him in the city, in Jerusalem, for they did not bring him into the tombs of the kings of Israel. And Hezekiah his son reigned in his place.*

Who could have seen what would happen next? His son Hezekiah was a good king, and there was revival under his reign. Who could have seen it coming? But the Lord knew. The Lord had made Micah for just such a time as this, and used him powerfully in that time.

God has ordained you for THIS moment, this place. You are not reading this book by accident. There's a reason why you have been taught what you've been taught and why you know what you know. Maybe things around you look darker than you've ever seen before. I cannot guarantee a revival. But I CAN guarantee that there is no level of wickedness— NONE—so great that God cannot pour out salvation on my country or on yours. Just because you can't see it coming doesn't mean He can't do it. I can also guarantee that where the people of God are found faithful with God's Word, GOD IS WELL-PLEASED. There was no revival under Jeremiah's ministry, but he was faithful. There WAS revival (eventually) under Micah's ministry, and he was faithful. Both of them pleased God.

We have our moment. We have our mission. We are God's people. And we have God's Word.

We have something else that God gave Micah. God gave Micah a friend. Micah's task was difficult, but not solitary. Isaiah was preaching at the same time, to the same city. Some refer to the book of Micah as a mini-Isaiah, because certain passages are very similar. That's not surprising. Both were giving God's Word in the same context with the same goal. But it also seems to indicate that these men interacted with each other. It would be shocking if they hadn't, since they were on the same mission.

These were two very different men. What an unlikely pair they were. Isaiah was older. His ministry started earlier. Isaiah preached during the reign of Jotham's father, Uzziah.

J. Sidlow Baxter said, "Isaiah was a man of the schools and Micah a man of the fields."[1]

Isaiah, from the statelier family, was the more sophisticated, and the better-known. This shows God's unlikely means as he joins two very different men together who came as partners to address the people of God during their generation. Each was a man for his times.

You and I are chosen for the time in which He has placed us. He has saved you and is ready to use you now, where you are. Do you believe that?

THE MESSAGE (1:1d)

Micah's message concerned judgment that would ultimately be followed by mercy. Although there are between nineteen and twenty-one separate oracles, they exist within three main messages, each beginning with language like that of a courtroom prosecution. He begins each main message by calling upon the people to HEAR Him.

> 1:2   *Hear you peoples, all of you.*
> 3:1   *And I said: Hear, you heads of Jacob and rulers of the house of Israel.*
> 6:1   *Hear what the LORD says.*

Each of these main messages moves from doom to hope. Each focuses on

- The just penalty that is coming because the people have violated the covenant
- God's faithfulness because He keeps covenant
- A future hope found in God's covenant promises.

Through Micah, God prosecutes His case against both the northern kingdom of Israel–and its power center Samaria, and against the southern kingdom of Judah–and its power center Jerusalem. God uses him to tell of

---

[1] J. Sidlow Baxter, *Explore the Book*, p. 187

the judgment of both, but he is especially a prophet to the southern kingdom, so his ministry is identified by the reigns of the kings of Judah.

This is the theme of the book: Judgment is coming in the present because of sin, but the future will hold blessing because of God's faithful covenant love.

So, in summary—

- We have a mission—The word of God has imparted that to us.
- We are each a man or a woman for that mission—God has saved us and given us His word.
- We each live in the moment we were ordained for—We are meant to serve in the times where we are.
- Our message is that judgment is coming, but that God delights in saving sinners. Our message for everyone is this: God's wrath is coming, but He offers forgiveness in Jesus who died for sinners and who rose from the dead. Run to Jesus and be saved from God's wrath. Meet Him as the God of mercy.

2
CAN YOU SEE GOD'S HAND?
(1:2-16)

How do you see what is going on in this world? Do you have the eyes to see God's hand in it all? In the news, you hear of something grievous going on. How do you process that?

Then, how do you see *your* world? Maybe you have something terrible going on that shakes you to the core. Do you have the eyes to see the hand of God in everything? You know it intellectually, but do you know it in your will and in your heart? Do you know that the God of the Bible really *does* exist, that He really *is* on His throne, that He really *is* involved in the affairs of this world and in the affairs of your life? Do you know that He's at work in this world judging sin and rewarding righteousness? Proverbs 14:34 says, *Righteousness exalts a nation, but sin us a reproach to any people.* Notice, the Lord's proverb there applies to *any* nation, to *any* people.

These verses in Micah remind us that this is our God. He is at work in this world and all its affairs.

Micah is preaching in dark days. The nation of Israel to the north is on the doorstep of Assyrian destruction. Judah to the south has been imitating the evil behavior of Israel. As a result, Judah is also on the brink of destruction. Micah declares judgment and doom because of the people's unfaithfulness to the covenant and because of God's faithfulness to execute the curses of the covenant. The people's sins are many, but at the root of all their sins is idolatry. They have forsaken the true and living God for gods that are not gods. Idolatry is erupting everywhere. If sin is like sickness, then the whole body is sick. Idolatry has produced a host of abominations. There is cultic prostitution. During the reign of King Ahaz, there is even the sacrifice of children. With idolatry have come social injustice, thievery and oppression. The leaders at every level are in on it—including the priests and the false prophets. It's reached the point where God is about to act, and He is announcing this fact through Micah.

GOD'S WITNESS AGAINST THE WORLD (1:2-4)

This is a courtroom scene. The Lord wants everyone to hear His testimony. The universe is His courtroom, and He is judge and prosecutor and witness, all at once. Notice what God shows us about Himself.

He is **transcendent**. He speaks from a vantage point that only He alone can testify from, His holy temple—in this context, from heaven itself. He sits on his heavenly throne over the entire world.

Psalm 11:4 *The LORD is in his holy temple;*
the LORD's throne is in heaven;
his eyes see, his eyelids test the children of man.

Before He gives His witness, He wants the world to hear Him in relationship to where they are. He is sovereign. He's not subject to His creatures; they are subject to Him. They will all answer to Him. He's the One who determines their future both as individuals and as nations. He raises up one nation and He puts down another. He is not a regional or tribal god. He is God over all, so he calls all peoples over the whole earth and everything in it to listen to Him.

He is **holy and just**. He is speaking from his holy throne. He's not asking for witnesses. He sees all, knows all and hears all. He can convict the world based upon His own complete, holy knowledge.

He is **immanent**. This is emphasized in verses 3 and 4. That is, He is not removed from the world that He has made. He is directly involved in the affairs of men. Micah warns that the Lord is *coming down*. He wants to paint a picture in our minds. He doesn't have to come down physically. He's already present, but in this way God's presence is envisioned.

He is **all-powerful**, able to judge all people's affairs. When He comes down in judgment, it's fearful. Micah pictures the world itself coming apart as God, like a great giant, takes His steps upon this planet. The mountains melt with the heat of His wrath, and the valleys split through the power of His presence. Men may think of the mountains as great and the valleys as deep, but to God they are nothing. Man's fortifications and strongholds will not stand for a moment when God comes down.

He is not coming down to deliver Israel. He is coming down in His holy *wrath*. Micah's contemporary, Isaiah, declared this same truth.

Isaiah 26:21 *For behold, the L*ORD *is coming out from his place to punish the inhabitants of the earth for their iniquity, and the earth will disclose the blood shed on it, and will no more cover its slain.*

Not many years earlier, the prophet Amos declared God's sovereignty over the earth by picturing Him as treading on it.

Amos 4:13 *For behold, he who forms the mountains and creates the wind, and declares to man what is his thought, who makes the morning darkness, and treads on the heights of the earth—the L*ORD*, the God of hosts, is his name!*

These mountains picture the high places of the earth. Whether he's speaking of fortresses and everything that people trust in, or whether he's speaking of the places of idolatry, God will crush them under His feet. It doesn't matter. Man's strength is as nothing when the Lord comes down. Who can resist Him?

There *is* a day in the future when the Lord is coming down to deliver. The Lord *is* coming to set His feet on this planet to set up His Kingdom, and the Lord is named Jesus, but that's not what Micah is describing here. This is a figurative picture of the Lord coming down, marching through the earth to deal with the sins of men. This is God's witness against the whole world, because He's sovereign over the whole world. Here's how Zechariah put it a couple of hundred years later:

Zechariah 14:1 *Behold, a day is coming for the L*ORD*, when the spoil taken from you will be divided in your midst. ² For I will gather all the nations against Jerusalem to battle, and the city shall be taken and the houses plundered and the women raped. Half of the city shall go out into exile, but the rest of the people shall not be cut off from the city. ³ Then the L*ORD *will go out and fight against those nations as when he fights on a day of battle. ⁴ On that day his feet shall stand on the Mount of Olives that lies before Jerusalem on the east, and the Mount of Olives shall be split in two from east to west by a very wide valley, so that one half of the Mount shall move northward, and the other half southward. ⁵ And you shall flee to the valley of my mountains, for the valley of the mountains shall reach to Azal. And you shall flee as* *you fled from the earthquake in the days of Uzziah king of Judah. Then the LORD my God will come, and all the holy ones with him.*

⁶ On that day there shall be no light, cold, or frost. ⁷ And there shall be a unique day, which is known to the LORD, neither day nor night, but at evening time there shall be light.

⁸ On that day living waters shall flow out from Jerusalem, half of them to the eastern sea and half of them to the western sea. It shall continue in summer as in winter.

⁹ And the LORD will be king over all the earth. On that day the LORD will be one and his name one.

GOD'S WITNESS IN THE JUDGMENT OF HIS PEOPLE (1:5-7)

Why is the Lord coming down out of His place? He says it's *for the transgression of Jacob and for the sins of the house of Israel.* Jacob refers to the ten northern tribes. Israel here refers to the southern kingdom. His judgment will begin with His people, His house. Because the Lord does not ignore the sins of even His own people, the world is on notice—God will not ignore its sin. Though God's people will know mercy in the end, He is allowing them to meet with the consequences of their own sin. It is a witness to the entire earth of God's holy justice and of the inescapability of guilt before His law.

Judgment against Samaria and Judah

Samaria (verse 5) is a picture of the covenant transgression by the whole northern kingdom. They are guilty before God. Then He speaks of Jerusalem. *"The high place of Judah is Jerusalem."* It's a picture of the idolatry that has gripped the whole southern nation. There are examples of this throughout the Minor Prophets. Occasionally there's a king who has a heart for God, like Jotham or Hezekiah. Even then, either the reforms fall short of what the Lord requires, or the reforms are not widespread.

Who will do this to Samaria? In 722, Samaria falls to Assyria, and people are deported. But through Micah, the Lord is emphasizing that *He* is doing this. God says, *"I will make Samaria a heap in the open country."* When you see the affairs of the world, or when you see the affairs of your life, do you have the eyes to see the hand of God?

Beginning in verse 6, he tells what Yahweh will do with Samaria. It will experience **total destruction** (1:6), as if the city was never there. Not all of that happened in 722, but it did happen later. It will experience **total reversal** of its sinful existence (1:7).

What she <u>would not do willingly</u> will be done forcibly. She wouldn't repent and get rid of *her carved images* and *her idols*, so the Lord will lay them waste.

What she <u>did willingly</u>, sold herself, will now be done to her. When it says she received her fees like a prostitute, there are a couple of possible meanings.

- It could point to the fact that in her practice of idolatry, she has supported cultic prostitution. Sexual immorality has gripped the land.
- It could also just be referring to the fact that she's played the harlot, and so she has tried to enrich herself like a prostitute. Someone will come and take it all away. The thing you have done with the thought of advancing yourself, now that thing will be done to you. With what they gather from you, they will do the same thing.

Bruce Waltke said

> Unbelieving secular humans see no connection between their immoral behavior and the cycles of depression, increasing crime, politicians instead of statesman to guide them, ceaseless war, and venereal diseases. If they would "see" God ruling earth's affairs, and tremble before him, they would have nothing to fear.[2]

Micah sees the hand of God guiding the foreign armies. We, too, should see God's hand in the world, because it is the truth.

GOD'S WEEPING PROPHET (1:8-16)

This judgment is a lamentation delivered through a weeping prophet.

A Picture of Exile, 1:8

He says, *For this I will lament and wail; I will go stripped and naked; I will make lamentation like the jackals, and mourning like the ostriches.* The word *ostriches* probably refers to the desert owl, so the thought is the howling of dog-like jackals and the screeching of the desert owl. He's heartbroken. Many are those who recognize the sins of our time, but where are the people who weep over them and are willing to rail against them? As Micah preaches

---

[2] Bruce K. Waltke, *A Commentary on Micah* (Grand Rapids: Wm. B. Eerdmans, 2007), p. 58

against sin, he's not gloating. He's grieving. In fact, he expresses himself as if already going into exile, lamenting, wailing and stripping himself naked.

The Lord used Micah's contemporary Isaiah to do the same. See Isaiah 20.

Isaiah 20 *In the year that the commander in chief, who was sent by Sargon the king of Assyria, came to Ashdod and fought against it and captured it—²at that time the LORD spoke by Isaiah the son of Amoz, saying, "Go, and loose the sackcloth from your waist and take off your sandals from your feet," and he did so, walking naked and barefoot.*

³Then the LORD said, "As my servant Isaiah has walked naked and barefoot for three years as a sign and a portent against Egypt and Cush, ⁴so shall the king of Assyria lead away the Egyptian captives and the Cushite exiles, both the young and the old, naked and barefoot, with buttocks uncovered, the nakedness of Egypt. ⁵Then they shall be dismayed and ashamed because of Cush their hope and of Egypt their boast. ⁶And the inhabitants of this coastland will say in that day, 'Behold, this is what has happened to those in whom we hoped and to whom we fled for help to be delivered from the king of Assyria! And we, how shall we escape?'"

A Picture of Suffering and A Memorable Warning (1:9-16))

He foresees a *wound* that's *incurable*. Micah, who lives in the south, declares that the wound of Samaria in the north has reached his own people. Maybe someone would hear him talk about Samaria and think, "Well, that's them." But Micah is saying, "No, this is you, too." The Lord has wounded Samaria and there's no recovering. Now it has come to Judah, to the very gate of Jerusalem.

Years later, Jeremiah uses the same kind of language.

Jeremiah 30:12 *For thus says the LORD:*
Your hurt is incurable,
*   and your wound is grievous.*
¹³There is none to uphold your cause,
*   no medicine for your wound,*
*   no healing for you.*
¹⁴All your lovers have forgotten you;
*   they care nothing for you;*
for I have dealt you the blow of an enemy,
*   the punishment of a merciless foe,*
because your guilt is great,

because your sins are flagrant.
¹⁵Why do you cry out over your hurt?
  Your pain is incurable.
Because your guilt is great,
  because your sins are flagrant,
  I have done these things to you.

In **1:10-16**, you find an extended section of word play, puns, word association, word definitions, and assonance—things that sound similar. He uses all these to drive home a point—pain is coming. (The Lord always wants us to really see what's in His Word and then to apply it.) Assyria captured 46 cities west of Jerusalem in 701 B.C. when Sennacherib marched right up to the city gates of Jerusalem. Micah uses word play concerning a handful of them to drive the point home. "Jerusalem, you have an incurable wound. You are on the doorstep of judgment yourself unless you listen and repent." This section is enclosed by verses 10 and 15, each reminding us of David.

- **Don't tell *Gath*** (1:10). This brings to mind David's lament upon the deaths of Saul and Jonathan.

  2 Samuel 1:20 *Tell it not in Gath, publish it not in the streets of Ashkelon, lest the daughters of the Philistines rejoice, lest the daughters of the uncircumcised exult.*

  Gath is the nearest Philistine town to land of God's people. The death of the Lord's anointed grieved David. How could he endure seeing the enemies of God exulting and rejoicing over the death of the king? Now Micah is saying the same thing; this grieves my heart. Don't tell it in Gath. Micah loathes the thought of God's enemies rejoicing.
- **Roll in the Dust, Dusttown** (1:10b).
  He then begins word associations. **Beth-le-aphrah** means house of dust. He says, *"roll yourselves in the dust."* The name of the little town is like an omen. House of Dust, roll in the dust, because this is what's coming.
- **The Place of Beauty Will Be Ugly** (1:11a). **Shaphir** means beauty or pleasant; and yet what he pictures is the opposite. *"Pass on your way, inhabitants of Beauty, inhabitants of Pleasant, in nakedness and shame."* The people will be marched out in ugly nakedness and shame.

- **Those Who Come Out, Won't** (1:11b). *Zaanan* sounds like the Hebrew word for "come out," but instead of coming to fight; they'll hide.

- **The House of Protection Won't Protect** (1:11c). *"The lamentation of Beth-ezel"*—which means house or temple of protection—*"shall take away from you its standing place."* There will be no place to stand there.

- **The Bitter Town Will Wait in Vain for Good** (1:12). *Maroth* means bitter or bitter fountain. They will wait in vain and will experience bitterness instead of hope. Good is not coming from the Lord, disaster is coming—all the way to the gates of Jerusalem. All these little towns to the west of Jerusalem are picturing what will happen with Sennacherib as he makes his way to the city gates of Jerusalem.

- **The City that Relied on Military Might Should Prepare to Flee** (1:13). *"Harness the steeds to the chariots, inhabitants of Lachish."* In Hebrew the word for "to the steeds" is "Larakesh." The word play is a matter of alliteration and assonance. Probably the thought concerning the steeds and the chariots is of fleeing. Lachish was fortified. It's as if Micah is saying, "You've put your confidence in your military might, but it won't do you any good. You might as well connect the horses to the chariots and get out of there."

He then tells us that Lachish was connected to Israel's sin. Lachish stands as a testimony of what's wrong, like a San Francisco or a Las Vegas. Kenneth Barker commented:

> It was one of the largest cities in Judah. It was located almost 30 miles southwest of Jerusalem and only 6 miles southwest of Moresheth-Gath. Rehoboam had fortified Lachish (2 Chr 11:19) so that it guarded the main approach to the capital city from that district. It had a massive city wall 20 feet thick and a defensive gateway comparable to the ones at Gezer, Hazor, and Megiddo. It was one of the last of the 46 cities to fall to Sennacherib in 701 B.C. (2Kgs 18:13, 2 Chr 32:9) The siege and the following procession of plunder are

depicted on the vast reliefs found in Sennacherib's palace at Nineveh.[3]

He gloried in taking this city.

- **The Betrothed City Is Taken Away** (1:14a). *Moresheth-gath* is next. *Moresheth* sounds like the Hebrew word for betrothed.

  > ...Since parting gifts were given to brides as dowries (1 Ki 9:16), it is possible that the designation is intended to convey that the town of Moresheth Gath is soon to be parted from Judah as a bride parts from her family.[4]

- **The Deceitful City Deceives** (1:14b). *Achzib* sounds like the Hebrew word for deceitful—Achzab. That word was used of a spring or a brook that would dry up in summer. In other words, the city will cease to exist. Your hopes for Achzib will prove to be deceitful. She won't be there long.[5]

- **The Conqueror City Will Be Conquered** (1:15a). *Mareshah* sounds like the Hebrew word for conqueror.

- **Israel's Glory Is Hidden** (1:15b) *The glory of Israel* which *shall come to* **Adullam** could be a reference to God marching through

---

[3] Barker, Kenneth L., "Micah" in *New American Commentary, volume 20: Micah, Nahum, Habakkuk, Zephaniah*, by Kenneth L. Barker and Waylon Bailey (Nashville: B&H Publishing Group, 1998), p. 59

[4] McComiskey, Thomas E. and Longman, Tremper III, "Micah" in *Expositors Bible Commentary vol. 8: Daniel-Malachi, Revised Edition*, Tremper Longman III and David Garland, general editors (Grand Rapids: Zondervan, 2008), p. 508)

[5] NET notes have a slightly different, possible interpretation: The place name *Achzib* (אַכְזִיב, 'akhziv, "place on the dried up river")... creates a word play on the similar sounding term כָּזָב (kazav, "lie, deception")... . Like the dried up river upon which its name was based, the city of Achzib would fail to help the kings of Israel in their time of need. ... Achzib will be as disappointing to the kings of Israel as a dried-up spring in the summer is to a thirsty traveler in the Jordanian desert. ... Because of the enemy invasion, *Achzib* would not be able to deliver soldiers for the army and/or services normally rendered to the crown.

these cities. His Hand is upon the Assyrian forces as these cities are gathered up one by one. But *the glory of Israel* here probably refers to their rulers coming to Adullam, so that Micah ends this section with another reminder of David. 1 Samuel 22:1-2 says, *David departed from there*—he was fleeing from Gath, fleeing from the Philistines—*and escaped to the cave of Adullam. And when his brothers and all his father's house heard it, they went down there to him. And everyone who was in distress, and everyone who was in debt, and everyone who was bitter in soul, gathered to him. And he became commander over them. And there were with him about four hundred men.* In other words, *the glory of Israel*, the rulers of Israel will go into hiding just as David hid in a cave in Adullam. In an unforgettable way for the people hearing him in their language, one by one, Micah takes these ominous names and associates them with the pain that is coming because of their sin. In this way, he is calling them to repentance.

His closing word (1:16) is *"Make yourselves bald and cut off your hair, for the children of your delight."* The delightful children are probably Jerusalem, Zion and Judah. They will grieve, shearing and shaving the head in mourning, and they'll look *as bald as the eagle.* The griffon vulture has a head and neck that appear bald. They will be heartbroken. Why? *For they shall go from you into exile.*

3
WOE TO THE OPPRESSORS
(2:1-5)

Micah's first chapter addressed direct sin against God, the sin of idolatry. When people replace the true God with gods of their own making, the result is utter chaos. The focus now changes to sin against people. When we sin against people, we're also sinning against God. We sometimes imagine that we can be right with God while we mistreat people. Here, the Lord makes clear that's not the case.

We've seen that the Lord is coming down in judgment. He'll begin with his own household. By doing that, He's sending a message to the whole world that He doesn't overlook sin. He's a God of perfect, holy justice.

THE SIN (2:1-2)

When God pronounces judgment through the prophets, it often begins, as here, with the Hebrew word "hoi"—woe, ah, alas. This word is sometimes used when people are mourning the dead, so one translation has "You are as good as dead." When Micah is declaring *woe*, it is a funeral dirge. The nation has sinned in such a way that God's judgment is at the doorstep.

Oppression

The sin being addressed is the sin of oppression, the heart of which was the sin of covetousness.

God hates oppression. We may have grown weary of hearing about oppression, because we live in a society in which there's a lot of exaggerated oppression. There are people who have first-world problems, who act as if they're being oppressed if they're not given something or if someone tells them "no." In our day, the subject of oppression is used to manipulate people. Even so, we cannot allow this to make us numb to the reality of oppression. God hates it. He won't overlook it. He will judge it. If you're reading this book and you're guilty of oppressing others, God hates that in your life. He hates it in the life of a nation that would excuse it—or, even worse, that would institutionalize it. He also hates it in the lives of preachers who won't speak about it—maybe because they're in on it, benefitting from the system. This is what we'll see in Micah 2.

As someone has pointed out, when God isn't valued, human life isn't valued. It shouldn't surprise us that in an idolatrous nation, abortion is excused. The love of people is taught by the love of God. Right treatment of people is based on God's righteous standards. Where covetousness abounds, chaos abounds, because men fight and war for what they want.

Remember this: sins do not commit themselves. Sins are committed by people. So, if you talk about the sin of oppression, you're talking about oppressors. That is why Micah describes the sinners in verse 1. *Woe to those*—to those people, those sinners—*who devise wickedness and work evil on their beds! When the morning dawns, they perform it, because it is in the power of their hand.*

He describes them in three ways. First, they're characterized by **wicked imaginations**. Psalm 1 tells us that godly people meditate on God's law day and night. That includes when they're resting. But these people rest by devising ways to advance themselves at the expense of others. Evil deeds are done in the heart before they are done with the hands.

Second, they are characterized by **wicked eagerness**. *When the morning dawns, they perform it.* The Hebrew word for *morning* here speaks of breaking light, perhaps even when stars are still visible in the night sky, but the light is just breaking forth. They get up early, ready to do the evil they've imagined. They can't wait to act on their plans. Are you like them, eager to do things that the Word of God identifies as sin?

Third, they're characterized by a **wicked conscience**. Why are they eager to do this evil? *Because it is in the power of their hand.* Because they can. For them, as one writer said, might is right.[6] They think, "If I have the power to

---

[6] Ragnar Redbeard, *Might is Right or the Survival of the Fittest* (London: W. J. Robbins, 5th Edition, 1910)

do it, then I'm going to do it." The only restraints on them are opportunity and ability. They're not restrained by love for God nor by love for people. They're not restrained by a sense of what's right and wrong. They're not restrained by a conscience informed by the Word of God. If they have the ability and the opportunity, they do wickedness.

In short, they have wicked imagination, wicked eagerness, and a wicked conscience. Their conscience now is seared, seemingly no longer to trouble them. They're up at dawn, ready to do the evil they've planned, because they can.

Next (2:2), Micah describes the covetousness that characterizes these oppressors.

Covetousness (2:2)

At the root of economic oppression is covetousness, a violation of the 10th Commandment.

Exodus 20:17 *You shall not covet your neighbor's house. You shall not covet your neighbor's wife, or his male servant, or his female servant, or his ox, or his donkey, or anything that is your neighbor's.*

God's law addresses both our actions and our desires. He says it is a sin to covet what your neighbor has—whether it's his house or his spouse, his servants or his possessions. When you covet, you are sinning.

Sin begins in the heart, in the desires. At times, we become numb to what is going on within our own hearts. We're quick to identify other people's sin, but slow to recognize ours, hiding within.

James Montgomery Boice wrote, "What does coveting mean? It means to want earnestly something you do not have, particularly something belonging to another person. It means not to be satisfied with what God has already given you. It means to be materialistic and greedy…The 10th Commandment reveals that sin is essentially a matter of the heart, for coveting is something that exists internally, long before it expresses itself in any outward action. How modern this all is. How keenly it strikes at the roots of our materialistic Western culture… We object to the sexual innuendos and come-ons in advertising, but even more pernicious is the ceaseless pitch for materialism, the constant temptation to covetousness. We are a generation of people never at peace with what we have, always seeking more. We are as guilty of coveting our neighbor's fields or houses or inheritance as were the citizens of Jerusalem."[7]

Why is covetousness a sin?

- Covetousness doesn't find its satisfaction in God. It always wants something more. Hebrews 13:5 warns against covetousness, then adds, *"for he has said, 'I will never leave you nor forsake you.' "* You can be satisfied with what you have, because He's there. He's enough. When we covet what someone else has, we are acting like we are deprived. That means we think God is not enough to satisfy our hearts. At the root of covetousness is idolatry.

- Covetousness doesn't trust God as an all-wise provider. His children can be content with what He's given. He knows what we need. God's Word teaches us to pray that He would give us neither too much nor too little.

> **Proverbs 30:8-9**...*Give me neither poverty nor riches;*
> *feed me with the food that is needful for me,*
> *lest I be full and deny you*
> *and say, "Who is the LORD?"*
> *or lest I be poor and steal*
> *and profane the name of my God.*

It's right for God to withhold from you that which He knows would put you in a place of great temptation. If you constantly strive after something God has not chosen to give you, you're really saying, "Lord, You don't know what's best for me. I need something that You've chosen not to give me." It means you think you're wise and God isn't.

- Covetousness doesn't allow us to love one other. It's present where love is absent. If I love you, I rejoice in what God has given you. I don't covet it. If my heart is free from covetousness, I can thank God for what He has chosen to entrust to you.

---

[7] Boice, James Montgomery, *The Minor Prophets, vol. 2: Micah – Malachi* (Grand Rapids: Baker Books, 2006)

WOE TO THE OPPRESSORS

- Covetousness isn't thankful for what it already has. It's ungrateful, blind to the blessings the Lord has provided, because it focuses on what it thinks it lacks.

- Covetousness wrongly assesses worth and ambition. What is real treasure? The world is full of people running after what they've identified as treasure, but it's not. They end up throwing away true riches in the pursuit of that which is only temporary, and which doesn't satisfy. They throw away their families, their churches, and their souls in the pursuit of that which isn't really riches. People may move far away for a higher-paying job. Then they ask, "Do you know of any church in that area?" They have things all wrong. Find your church, then move there. Then drive to work if you must, because your soul is more important than your paycheck. When we always want something more, we don't understand what's really valuable, so our ambitions are misguided. As the Apostle Paul said, *"Therefore, we also have as our ambition, whether at home or absent, to be pleasing to Him"* (2 Corinthians 5:9). That's your goal as a believer.

- Covetousness is at the root of a host of other sins. It buries itself. It hides. Many of our sins flow from it, but when we see them, we don't immediately think, "You know what's at the root of this sin? It's that my heart is not satisfied with God. The root of this sin is that I am committing the sin of idolatry. It's that I'm covetous."

THE SENTENCE (2:3-5)

Symmetrical punishment

God pronounces the sentence for the oppressors, and it is poetic justice. There is appropriate symmetry in His judgments. It's done with **planning.** The oppressors devised evil upon their beds – God devised disaster for them in return. It's done with **power.** The oppressors dealt with others according to their power – God will put them under the yoke of foreigners. It's done with **humiliation.** The oppressors humiliated their victims – God will put them under a yoke that takes away their haughty posture. It's done with **mocking.** The oppressors mocked those whom they robbed – God will see to it that their enemies mock them. It's done with **removal of inheritance.** The oppressors robbed others of their inheritance – God will take them away so that they do not have anyone left to apportion an inheritance.

<u>These are strong words, and they were being proclaimed through the prophet Micah</u>. As will always be the case when God's Word goes forth, there were some who did not acknowledge the true origin of Micah's message. They could not see the hand of God at work through the mouth of this prophet, because they did not WANT TO BELIEVE that what he said was actually God's Word. We'll see that in the next section.

4
RELIGIOUS OPPOSITION
(2:6-11)

If you're preaching truth, some of the most vicious opposition you will ever face will come from those who claim to represent the same God you do. True preachers face opposition from those who lie in the name of the true God. We are reminded of that in these verses.

THE RESISTANCE (2:6-11)

They do not want to believe what Micah is saying. They have a vested interest in their religious activity. They can't "let him go on like this." Remember the resistance that Jesus met when He came to this earth. *"If we let him go on like this, everyone will believe in him, and the Romans will come and take away both our place and our nation"* (John 11:48).

The preachers who resist Micah (2:6-7a)

There are false prophets—false preachers standing in opposition to the true prophets of God.

They want Micah's preaching to stop (6a). Why would they want that?

It threatens their reputations. His preaching doesn't match theirs, so it's an indictment of them. If he is telling the truth, then they are spiritual liars.

It also threatens their goals, the goals of their preaching. Why are these false prophets declaring peace when there is no peace? It serves them with the rich and the powerful. It keeps them in places of influence. The nation's leaders use the false prophets as cheerleaders for the way things are.

Tied to the first and second reasons, it threatens <u>their positions</u>. If the people believe Micah, the false prophets will lose their place. Thus, they want him to be quiet.

For a similar example, see the story of Micaiah (a century earlier) in 1 Kings 22. Ahab thought the problem was with the messenger and with the message, not with himself. The false prophet Zedekiah also opposed Micaiah, and was very theatrical and even physically violent about it.

They paint his preaching as inappropriate and untrue (2:6b). Hoping to shut him up, they attack him. They paint his preaching as both inappropriate (*One should not preach of such things*) and untrue (*shame will not overtake us*).

No doubt, they painted Micah's preaching as dangerous—as a betrayal of the nation. Like King Ahab, they said no disaster was coming. The spiritual schemes of our enemy never change. The same sort of attack is leveled against preachers of the truth today. "This is inappropriate—dangerous— hateful—divisive! People shouldn't say such things. This is unacceptable in polite society."

They deny his preaching with their understanding of God (2:7a). Micah identifies some of the statements being made by the false prophets and points out whose speech is truly inappropriate.

They say Micah preaches a false view of God. "Micah's preaching says Yahweh is impatient, but He isn't." In other words, God is a God of love and mercy, but not judgment. He does not judge in the ways that Micah says.

The false prophets still love to talk about grace and mercy. They present a god who never really deals with sin—in fact, they eventually deny the biblical concepts of sin—so that their god is a god of perverted love and perverted grace.

We live in a time of grace perversion. "Gospel-centered" is, FOR SOME, code for a grace-only message. "Don't talk about sin; don't talk about obedience; don't talk about judgment. That's legalism. Just talk about GRACE." This perversion often occurs in times when God's judgment is upon a nation. You find it in the mouths of preachers who don't want to believe that God judges.

The most dangerous kind of preaching today is preaching that sounds right on the gospel, but distorts the effects of the gospel.

Titus 2:11-13 *The grace of God … [is] training us to renounce ungodliness and worldly passions, and to <u>live self-controlled, upright and godly lives in the present age</u>.*

God's grace calls you to live a holy life. His Word contains imperatives, not just indicatives. We're called to hear the imperatives and to obey them. Anyone who tells you otherwise is lying to you, distorting and perverting grace.

When there's an outbreak of the perversion of grace in lands that are under the judging hand of God, people want to believe in a God who <u>doesn't judge</u>. Where there's an outbreak of <u>sin</u> in a land and everyone wants to embrace their sin, people want to believe in a God who wouldn't deal with us for our sins, who wouldn't scourge us as God promises He does with every son whom He receives. Such teaching is a perversion of what the Bible teaches about sanctification.

MICAH'S RESPONSE TO THE PEOPLE AND AGAINST THE FALSE PROPHETS (2:7-11)

How does Micah respond to this attack?

Micah's words are only disaster for the disobedient (2:7b). If someone does what's right, Micah's preaching does good to them. God promises forgiveness, mercy, and blessing to those who will heed him and repent.

Micah's words declare war on those who wage war (2:8-9). He points out that the oppressive acts taking place in the land are acts of war against their own people. <u>They wage war on unsuspecting men</u> (2:8), stripping off their rich robes as those losing a battle might be stripped. <u>They wage war on women</u> (2:9a), driving them out from their delightful houses. He may have been referring to widows. <u>They wage war on children</u> (2:9b), robbing them of the inheritance God had assigned to them.

Some of these actions may have been legal, at least as they interpreted their law, but they were not righteous. Not everything that men make legal is righteous. Abortion may be legal right now, but it's not righteous. Homosexual marriage may be legal, but it's not righteous.

Micah's words point to the ruinous effects of sin (2:10).

<u>The land of rest will provide them no rest</u>.

God promised the land to them as a place of rest. (See Deut. 12:8-10, for example.) Because of the people's sin and Moses' sin, the Lord swore in His wrath, "They will not enter My rest." (See Deut. 1:34-38; Psalm 95:11.) They missed the promised rest, but their children entered it.

Now the Lord is saying through Micah, *"This is no place to rest."* They are going into exile. Why? Because of their *uncleanness that destroys with a grievous destruction.*

The land God gave them has been ruined by their sins.

They think the land is theirs to do with as they please. They can rob people of clothing and houses and inheritances, because they don't recognize that the Lord assigned these things. They're taking from the children the Lord's splendor, what He has given. This is His people, His land, an inheritance assigned by God, and they act as if it's theirs. So, they won't be allowed to keep it. They were to be a light to the nations (Isa. 42:6; 49:6), but they've become a force for evil. The Lord will not tolerate it.

Micah's words diagnose the real problem (2:11). Micah gets to the root of the issue. How did they get to this point? By rejecting the Word of God. They don't want it. They find it intolerable. They love empty words (winds and lies).

They love to hear someone *preach of wine and strong drink.* There are a couple of ways you could take that. One is that they love affirming words—the kind of preaching that gives them permission and affirmation when they indulge their sinful passions. The other way to take this is that they love delusional words—preaching that's like wine and strong drink, numbing them to the truth. They want a message that inebriates them, putting them to sleep even as the sword of God's wrath is dangling over their heads.

They love preachers who fit their sinful condition. Micah says this kind of preacher *would be the preacher for this people!* What does he mean? This applies two ways. First, this is the kind of preacher you would choose. Second, this is the kind of preacher you deserve. It is God's judgment upon a people when he lets them have preachers who say only what the people want to hear instead of preaching God's Word.

Is there *anyone* who can change this picture? Yes. We've already noted that by God's grace, Hezekiah comes on the scene. The Lord works in that king's heart through Micah's preaching (Jer. 26:18-19). There is a revival in the southern kingdom, and the Lord spares them for more than 100 years.

Can the ugly picture of oppression change? Yes. How? By God's grace. Only God can change such a situation, but He can change it. When His

Word goes forth, God grants ears to hear, eyes to see, and a heart that feels. Through His Word and His Spirit, He causes men to run to Him by running to His Son Jesus, the only Savior. Only God grants that, and He <u>can</u> grant it.

If you believe our world is so far gone that God can't save sinners in droves, you don't know the power of our God nor the power of the gospel. We are all tempted to grumble and complain about our world. Instead, pray for it and preach God's truth to it. Preach the whole Word of God.

These people deserved a preacher who would talk about strong drink and wine. But God sent them a preacher who wouldn't be silenced and who declared the true God. The Lord worked. Like Israel in Micah's day, we don't need the kind of preachers our world deserves. We need those the Lord has equipped, called and given the gospel.

In a sense, every Christian has a preaching ministry somewhere. It may not be behind a pulpit, but people hear what's said. We must proclaim the gospel. As we do, we must remember that *we* don't save sinners. *God* saves sinners, and He is powerful to save sinners. May we be faithful with the Word He's entrusted to us, believing in His ability, not our own.

5
HOPE IN DESPAIR
(2:12-13)

Up to this point in the Book of Micah, the scene has been one of utter darkness. Through Micah, the Lord has painted the picture of a land that's full of idolatry, leading to covetousness, leading to oppression. People's houses and lands and inheritances are being stolen by means that may have been legal, but not righteous. People were being robbed due to the strategies that were formed in the minds of the wicked as they would lie in their beds at night.

And there was no help from the religious realm. The false prophets said Micah's preaching was inappropriate. They said the Lord wasn't like what Micah said.

It was a dark, dark time. What would it feel like to live in such a time? Many of us live in a similar time. We live in a nation that has gone from tolerating sin, to being saturated with sin, to embracing and celebrating sin. Things God calls sin—whether it's homosexual activity or abortion or a wicked, godless view of man's origins or something else—are now seen as things to be applauded, and the embracing of those things is called a virtue.

How does it feel to serve the Lord in such a time? Both Isaiah and Micah gave voice to what we may feel.

Isaiah 57:1-2 *The righteous man perishes, and no one lays it to heart; devout men are taken away, while no one understands.*

For the righteous man is taken away from calamity; he enters into peace;
    they rest in their beds who walk in their uprightness.

He's describing righteous people, godly people dying. Their death is pictured as sleep. They escape the calamity. They have gone into peace as they now are in the presence of God. But here's the sad thing: no one understands the value of these people who are dying. No one takes to heart what the loss of such people means.

Micah 7:2 *The godly has perished from the earth,*
    and there is no one upright among mankind;
they all lie in wait for blood,
    and each hunts the other with a net.

We are living, he says, in violent times, times of chaos. Where are godly people? It seems like they're disappearing. Maybe you've felt like that. Is there hope in such a time? Yes.

As we saw in the introduction to Micah, the book has three main messages consisting of about 21 different oracles. Each main message is organized the same way. It begins with a message of doom and ends with a message of hope. In each case **that hope is found in the promises of God,** promises made in God's covenants with His people throughout the Old Testament. Our hope, too, is in the future that God has promised by His grace to a people whom He saves. As the first main message of Micah is brought to its conclusion here in verses 12 and 13, we see hope based on three promises from the Lord.

The promise of a remnant (God has a plan for ethnic Israel) (2:12)

God makes reference to a remnant. In the book of Micah, *Jacob* and *Israel* refer to the nation in its ideal sense, without political division. Yahweh promises that he will *assemble, gather, set together* His people.

A remnant means God still has a plan. If the Lord is going to bring His people together, they will still exist. So, the judgments that Micah has been describing do not mean the obliteration of ethnic Israel. The offspring of the patriarchs will survive. They have a future, and there is a believing remnant in that future.

The emphasis here is on a physical remnant, but the Bible clearly teaches the truth of a spiritual remnant as well. Within the nation of Israel—ethnic Israel—God saves some, reserves them and keeps them in faith. He preserves a people who know Him, who will glorify Him and speak the truth about Him. Even in the darkest of times, the Lord is saving people and preserving them.

The apostle Paul wrote this same truth many years later in the book of Romans—that God saves an Israel within Israel.

Romans 9 *I am speaking the truth in Christ—I am not lying; my conscience bears me witness in the Holy Spirit— ² that I have great sorrow and unceasing anguish in my heart. ³ For I could wish that I myself were accursed and cut off from Christ for the sake of my brothers, my kinsmen according to the flesh. ⁴ They are Israelites, and to them belong the adoption, the glory, the covenants, the giving of the law, the worship, and the promises. ⁵ To them belong the patriarchs, and from their race, according to the flesh, is the Christ, who is God over all, blessed forever. Amen.*

⁶ But it is not as though the word of God has failed. For not all who are descended from Israel belong to Israel, ⁷ and not all are children of Abraham because they are his offspring, but "Through Isaac shall your offspring be named." ⁸ This means that it is not the children of the flesh who are the children of God, but the children of the promise are counted as offspring. ⁹ For this is what the promise said: "About this time next year I will return, and Sarah shall have a son."

He's obviously talking about ethnic Israelites. Paul knows the discouragement in his heart as he watches the vast majority of his people reject Jesus as Messiah. He's thinking through that issue in Romans 9-11, asking what this means in terms of God's plan for ethnic Israel, Paul's kinsmen according to the flesh.

To be an Israelite indeed means you know the living God. It means you accept and know the Messiah. There is an Israel within Israel. That truth didn't just begin in the New Testament. Both Isaiah (10:21) and Micah speak of the remnant.

This is a very encouraging truth. God's people often suffer in God's judgments along with the unbelievers, but they aren't regarded the same. The Lord knows those who are His. He never forgets them. Elijah was reminded that the Lord had preserved 7,000 who had not bowed the knee to Baal.

Paul took the truth of the remnant and applied it to his own time in the first century.

Romans 11 *I ask, then, has God rejected his people? By no means! For I myself am an Israelite, a descendant of Abraham, a member of the tribe of Benjamin. ² God has not rejected his people whom he foreknew. Do you not know what the Scripture says of Elijah, how he appeals to God against Israel? ³ "Lord, they have killed your prophets, they have demolished your altars, and I alone am left, and they seek my life." ⁴ But what* *is God's reply to him? "I have kept for myself seven thousand men who have not bowed the knee to Baal."* [5] *So too at the present time there is a remnant, chosen by grace.*

He's not at all saying that God has no plan for ethnic Israel, that all of that has been fulfilled in the church. The word *remnant* there has no meaning if the Lord has no more plans for ethnic Israel. However, the emphasis here in Micah 2 is more on physical preservation, pointing to what the Lord will do in the future. The Lord promises a remnant.

The bold promise of a future for that remnant (2:12b-13)

God not only indicates that there will be a **remnant,** He promises a **future** for them.

He promises to *assemble* and *gather* them. The Lord will bring the remnant together. This, of course, assumes a scattering. In some way, the people of God are separated from one another, scattered, and the living God will then bring them together. It will be a significant gathering, because it's *like a flock in its pasture, a noisy multitude of men.*

He promises to deliver them. The Lord will *set them together like sheep in a fold, like a flock in its pasture.* There's some sort of enclosure, and some sort of danger.

He promises to lead them. The Lord will be the one who *opens the breach* to lead them safely out of their enclosure. He's pictured as a shepherd (yet king) who breaks open the enclosure, and they pass by Him. He then passes to the front of the flock and leads them.

Historical Context

As is often the case with prophecy, Micah's words have both a near fulfillment and a distant fulfillment.

The deliverance from Assyria in 701 BC. This was in the very near future. In 701 B.C. the Assyrian king, Sennacherib, would march through Micah's land, taking cities and villages, making his way to Jerusalem, which he would then besiege. When those cities southwest of Jerusalem were taken by the Assyrians, thousands of people who fled from them ended up in Jerusalem. They were all gathered together and enclosed. When you pay a ransom to the devil, don't be surprised when the devil wants more. Sennacherib threatened Hezekiah. His demand was full, unconditional surrender.

2 Kings 18:13-15 *In the fourteenth year of King Hezekiah, Sennacherib king of Assyria came up against all the fortified cities of Judah and took them.* ¹⁴ *And Hezekiah king of Judah sent to the king of Assyria at Lachish, saying, "I have done wrong; withdraw from me. Whatever you impose on me I will bear." And the king of Assyria required of Hezekiah king of Judah three hundred talents of silver and thirty talents of gold.* ¹⁵ *And Hezekiah gave him all the silver that was found in the house of the* LORD *and in the treasuries of the king's house.*

The ransom didn't satisfy Sennacherib. He wanted complete surrender. Hezekiah was devastated. He poured out his heart in prayer to the Lord, then turned to the prophet Isaiah who said, *Thus says the Lord: Do not be afraid….* The Lord heard Hezekiah's prayer. See 2 Kings 18 and 19. Notice God's answer concerning Sennacherib, given through Isaiah to Hezekiah after Hezekiah prayed.

2 Kings 19:25 *"Have you not heard*
  that I determined it long ago?
I planned from days of old
  what now I bring to pass,
that you should turn fortified cities
  into heaps of ruins,
²⁶ *while their inhabitants, shorn of strength,*
  are dismayed and confounded,
and have become like plants of the field
  and like tender grass,
like grass on the housetops,
  blighted before it is grown.

²⁷ *But I know your sitting down*
  and your going out and coming in,
  and your raging against me.
²⁸ *Because you have raged against me*
  and your complacency has come into my ears,
I will put my hook in your nose
  and my bit in your mouth,
and I will turn you back on the way
  by which you came.

²⁹ *"And this shall be the sign for you: this year eat what grows of itself, and in the second year what springs of the same. Then in the third year sow and reap and plant vineyards, and eat their fruit.* ³⁰ *And the surviving remnant of the house of Judah shall again take root downward and bear fruit upward.* ³¹ *For out of Jerusalem shall go a remnant, and out of Mount Zion a band of survivors. The zeal of the* LORD *will do this.*

[32] "Therefore thus says the LORD concerning the king of Assyria: He shall not come into this city or shoot an arrow there, or come before it with a shield or cast up a siege mound against it. [33] By the way that he came, by the same he shall return, and he shall not come into this city, declares the LORD. [34] For I will defend this city to save it, for my own sake and for the sake of my servant David."

Jerusalem has been filling up with thousands of refugees. The Lord is gathering them together there like sheep in a fold, enclosed by the Assyrians. The Lord says he will turn Assyria back around to where they came from. He will save His people.

It's based on covenants, on promises God has made. Those promises do not hinge on the merits of ethnic Israel. He <u>never chose them based upon their merits</u>. He <u>doesn't keep these promises based upon their merits</u>. God will do what He does for His own name's sake.

2 Kings 19:35 *And that night the angel of the LORD went out and struck down 185,000 in the camp of the Assyrians. And when people arose early in the morning, behold, these were all dead bodies. [36] Then Sennacherib king of Assyria departed and went home and lived at Nineveh.*

There you have it—the remnant of Israel like sheep in a pen in the city of Jerusalem, an enemy outside the gates. It seems like there's no deliverance. The living God frees them. The Lord tells about it before He does it, through the prophet Micah.

The return from exile after the Babylonian captivity. Others see in this the regathering of the people following the Babylonian captivity. God gathered His people back into their land in amazing ways.

An end-times deliverance when the Messiah returns. In prophecies like this, we also see promises that find an ultimate fulfillment in the personal presence of the Messiah at His second coming. Just as there were believing people in Micah's day, so there will be believing people in the days to come. Their God will know them, and He will know where they are, and He will gather them together. There will be a believing Israel.

Deuteronomy 30:1 *"And when all these things come upon you, the blessing and the curse, which I have set before you, and you call them to mind among all the nations where the LORD your God has driven you, [2] and return to the LORD your God, you and your children, and obey his voice in all that I command you today, with all your heart and with all your soul, [3] then the LORD your God will restore your fortunes and have mercy on you, and he will gather you again from all the peoples where the LORD your God has scattered you. [4] If your outcasts are in the uttermost parts of heaven, from there the LORD your God will gather you, and from there he will take you. [5] And the LORD your God* *will bring you into the land that your fathers possessed, that you may possess it. And he will make you more prosperous and numerous than your fathers. ⁶ And the LORD your God will circumcise your heart and the heart of your offspring, so that you will love the LORD your God with all your heart and with all your soul, that you may live. ⁷ And the LORD your God will put all these curses on your foes and enemies who persecuted you. ⁸ And you shall again obey the voice of the LORD and keep all his commandments that I command you today. ⁹ The LORD your God will make you abundantly prosperous in all the work of your hand, in the fruit of your womb and in the fruit of your cattle and in the fruit of your ground. For the LORD will again take delight in prospering you, as he took delight in your fathers, ¹⁰ when you obey the voice of the LORD your God, to keep his commandments and his statutes that are written in this Book of the Law, when you turn to the LORD your God with all your heart and with all your soul.*

This is just one text of many that make the same promises to Israel. These all flow out the promises made to Abraham. The Spirit of God make this abundantly clear through what the apostle Paul wrote concerning Israel.

Romans 11:15 *For if their rejection means the reconciliation of the world, what will their acceptance mean but life from the dead?*

The Lord is saving Gentiles in great numbers today; *the reconciliation of the world.* When we look at most of ethnic Israel, we see *their rejection.* In the future, there will be *their acceptance,* which will be like a seemingly impossible resurrection.

Romans 11:16 *If the dough offered as firstfruits is holy, so is the whole lump, and if the root is holy, so are the branches.*

¹⁷ *But if some of the branches were broken off, and you, although a wild olive shoot, were grafted in among the others and now share in the nourishing root of the olive tree, ¹⁸ do not be arrogant toward the branches. If you are, remember it is not you who support the root, but the root that supports you. ¹⁹ Then you will say, "Branches were broken off so that I might be grafted in." ²⁰ That is true. They were broken off because of their unbelief, but you stand fast through faith. So do not become proud, but fear. ²¹ For if God did not spare the natural branches, neither will he spare you. ²² Note then the kindness and the severity of God: severity toward those who have fallen, but God's kindness to you, provided you continue in his kindness. Otherwise you too will be cut off. ²³ And even they, if they do not continue in their unbelief, will be grafted in, for God has the power to graft them in again. ²⁴ For if you were cut from what is by nature a wild olive tree, and grafted, contrary to nature, into a cultivated olive tree, how much more will these, the natural branches, be grafted back into their own olive tree.*

²⁵ *Lest you be wise in your own sight, I do not want you to be unaware of this mystery, brothers: a partial hardening has come upon Israel, until the fullness of the Gentiles has come in. ²⁶ And in this way all Israel will be saved, as it is written,*

"The Deliverer will come from Zion,
  he will banish ungodliness from Jacob";
²⁷ "and this will be my covenant with them
  when I take away their sins."

There is coming a great outpouring of salvation upon ethnic Israelites. Remember that God's choice of ethnic Israel was not based on merit. God chose them in order to display His own character and abilities. This does not in any way diminish the oneness that God's people experience in the church. This does not God diminish God's plan for the salvation of Gentiles that was expressed from the very beginning in the Abrahamic covenant. This simply displays God's ability to work out specific displays of His beautiful grace in the midst of a grand picture. God has a plan for ethnic Israelites. God has a plan for nations in a future millennial Kingdom, and in this way, God will put on display the full beauty of His saving grace.

Often, people want to take a beautiful portrait full of nuance and many different colors and then flatten it out and make it all one generic picture, but it's not. God is putting on display the fullness of the beauty of His power and His grace in salvation. That's why He made promises and why He will keep those promises.

Deuteronomy 7:7 *It was not because you were more in number than any other people that the LORD set his love on you and chose you [Israel], for you were the fewest of all peoples, ⁸ but it is because the LORD loves you and is keeping the oath that he swore to your fathers, that the LORD has brought you out with a mighty hand and redeemed you from the house of slavery, from the hand of Pharaoh king of Egypt.*

So, looking back at our two verses, we see the promise of a remnant and the promise of a future for that remnant. The Lord will gather them. He will deliver them. He will lead them. It found an immediate fulfillment in the deliverance from the Assyrians in 701 B.C., but it points to something even greater that the Lord will do through the Lord Jesus Christ in the future.

The promise of the Deliverer for the remnant

In these two verses, in addition to the promise of a remnant and the promise of a future for that remnant, we observe the promise of the Deliverer for that remnant. Here, God describes Himself in four pictures. They find their full expression in the Lord Jesus Christ.

He is a shepherd. The people of God are gathered *like sheep*; they are cared for and led. He will open the breach and lead them out.

He is a captain. The fact that He *opens the breach* and leads them out in face of great opposition is a picture of a great captain, a great warrior. He stands at their head as one who has set them free.

He is a king. *Their king passes on before them.* He is their ruler, their sovereign. He is the authority in their lives.

He is Lord. This picture captures the other three. *Their king passes on before them.* Who is this king? *The LORD at their head.* All of these pictures find their clearest expression in the Lord Jesus Christ. He is our shepherd, captain, king and is Himself the LORD.

There is hope for us.

Do you find yourself discouraged by dark days like Micah's? Do you wonder where the godly man has gone?

2 Timothy 2:19 *But God's firm foundation stands, bearing this seal: "The Lord knows those who are his" and "Let everyone who names the name of the Lord depart from iniquity."*

There **is** hope. Here it is: *The Lord knows those who are His.* You may suffer alongside the ungodly in the midst of a nation in decline, but the Lord knows those who are His, and He has a future for them. He's told us what our future is. His Kingdom is not of this world. This affliction is momentary. The glory ahead is eternal.

You, Christian, are a missionary. You are a citizen of heaven on loan to this world, serving on a mission for the Lord Jesus Christ as God gathers in the elect through the preaching of the gospel. One day we'll all be gathered together in the presence of our Great Shepherd. He will deliver us from this age of evil and He will rule over us and feed us and care for us for forever. We have a Champion. We have a Shepherd. We have a Captain. We have a King. We have the Lord.

We once belonged to the domain of darkness, trapped in our sin. We had no strength to set ourselves free. But the Lord Jesus Christ came from heaven to earth, lived a sinless life, and died on the cross to be our Deliverer. He was raised from the dead and lives forevermore. There was a day, in your darkness, when God said, "Let there be light" and the light of the gospel of Jesus Christ broke into your darkness. The chains fell off, the jail door was opened, and you walked out free. He freed you. Now He shepherds you and rules your life. The same One who delivered you individually will deliver us collectively. We will live in His presence forever, and the full display of God's glorious grace will be seen—Jew and Gentile saved by God's grace. Praise God for His glorious grace!

6
DISASTROUS LEADERS
(3:1-12)

The leaders of a people can be both a <u>judgment</u> from God and a <u>reason</u> for judgment. That is, God often judges a people by giving them the leaders they deserve. But it's a vicious cycle, because those same leaders lead in paths that would invite more acts of judgment from God. He raises up kings and kingdoms and removes them. Through all of this, God demonstrates truth to the world.

Proverbs 14:34 *Righteousness exalts a nation,*
but sin is a reproach to any people.

That proverb does not express a blind principle. The principle of sowing and reaping is not a blind law operating on its own. God is active. He blesses unrighteousness and punishes sin.

Micah is preaching to a people on the brink of disaster. What is taking place in Israel is both a <u>reflection</u> of judgment and an <u>invitation</u> for judgment. The fact that their leadership is so corrupt demonstrates God's refusal to bless a land that has given itself to corruption, so He has given them leaders that they deserve.

At the same time, those leaders commit the sins that call for additional acts of judgment. God has sent Micah to declare this, to reprove these leaders, and to call for repentance. In a nation that has been ordained by God to represent Him, the leadership is not just of political nature. In this passage, God is addressing first the rulers and then the religious leaders.

This begins the second of the three major messages in Micah. It again follows the form of a legal indictment. God begins by calling upon everybody to **listen**. 3:1: *Hear, you heads of Jacob and rulers of the house of Israel!* He goes on to address the prophets and the priests as well. God is calling upon the whole world, if you recall from chapter 1, to hear Him as He functions as witness, as prosecutor, and as judge. Prosecuting His case through the prophet Micah, God Himself bears witness to what He sees and knows, and then God pronounces His judgment on such deeds.

God's witness against the rulers (3:1-4)

These verses describe disastrous leadership, the kind of leaders who lead a people into disaster. The opening words of the first verse remind us that God is using a human instrument to give His Word. He begins by indicting the people's *heads* and *rulers*.

James Montgomery Boice wrote, "Undoubtedly, it was common to use the words 'leaders and rulers' for administrators of justice as well as political figures. These justices were probably the leaders of houses or families. In Exodus 18, Moses appointed leaders from the various tribes, houses, and families to be a system of courts for minor crimes. No doubt, Judah had a similar court system."[8]

These are the leaders of the political and legal systems, the ones who set the nation's course. The Lord has two things to say to them and then to the religious leaders: Here are your sins, and here is what I am going to do about them.

The indictment (3:1-3): The people's rulers oversee a system characterized by **gross injustice**. He asks them a question that applies as much to leaders in our time as it did theirs: *Is it not for you to know justice?* Isn't it the responsibility of those who oversee justice to know what justice is? The point is not that they would know what it is intellectually, but that they would be committed to justice. Justice is a theme of this passage. The word appears three times in this chapter. A healthy land's leaders are committed to true justice. They defend what's right and punish what's wrong. A nation is headed for disaster when right and wrong are inverted. Israel's leaders have **perverted justice**. They have inverted good and evil. *"You hate the good and you love the evil"* (3:2).

---

[8] Boice, James Montgomery, *The Minor Prophets: Micah – Malachi* (Grand Rapids: Kregel, 1996), p. 29

Not only do they pervert justice. They **devour** people. He pictures them as cannibals (3:2-3). These leaders are wicked and cruel, punishing the right. They reward the wrong without mercy.

The judgment (3:4): The Lord knows that they pay no attention to the ruin they bring about in the lives of the people. The Lord pronounces judgment.

A day will come when they are in trouble. They will cry out to the Lord, because they imagine that they're still on the Lord's side. But they will find no mercy because *they have made their deeds evil.*

God's witness against the religious leaders (3:5-7)

God does not just indict the rulers. He also indicts the religious leaders.

The indictment (3:5)

In general – They lead God's people astray. They are false guides and dangerous leaders, because to follow them spiritually results in devastation. It's like what Jesus said about the Pharisees who were offended at his teaching: *Let them alone; they are blind guides. And if the blind lead the blind, both will fall into a pit* (Matt. 15:14). Each has his own responsibility in this. False prophets and false teachers will bear a heavy load on the day of judgment, but those who follow them also have responsibility. We are responsible to measure what we hear by the Word of God, holding on to what's good and walking in what's true.

In specific terms – They are prophets for profit. They lead people astray, giving people the kind of preaching they desire. These are prophets for hire, working to enrich themselves, which means that these are pretended spokesmen for God. As one commentator put it, "Money speaks louder than God" to these prophets.[9] They are listening for the sound of money, and voices that they can respond to, in order to enrich themselves. They *cry "Peace"* to those who give them something to sink their teeth into (vs 5). (He uses a verb that in this form usually refers to the deadly bite of a serpent.[10] Did he use this word to remind us of the true spiritual nature of these men?) They are teachers proclaiming the imaginations of their own mind, and what guides their message is their desire for their own benefit. When a nation is spiritually ill, that shows up not only in its political leaders

---

[9] Elwell, Walter A., *Evangelical Dictionary of Biblical Theology*, "Micah, Theology of." (Grand Rapids: Baker Book House, 1996)

[10] Crossway Bibles, *The ESV Study Bible* (Wheaton, IL: Crossway Bibles, 2008), 1700

and its <u>judicial</u> leaders, but also in its <u>religious</u> leaders. You find a host of false preachers and teachers who are enriching themselves in the name of God, who cry *"Peace, peace"* when there is no peace (see Jer 6:14).

Today we see both corrupt leaders and corrupt preachers. We have the kinds of leaders our society deserves. They <u>openly reject</u> the living God, His Word and His standards, reflecting our sinfulness. At the same time, the land is full of men enriching themselves in the name of God, preaching not the Scriptures, not truth, but their own "truth"—which is really a lie. They are blind leaders of the blind, leading them straight into disaster while they say, "All is peaceful and all is well if you give me more money and buy my latest book!"

The judgment (3:6-7)

Their judgment will match their crime. <u>They will meet with *darkness*.</u> They were meant to be instruments of God for distributing light. Instead, they proclaimed their own imaginations. That is darkness. <u>*The sun will go down* on them—they will be finished.</u> They are already in darkness, but God will make it apparent. <u>They will *be disgraced*.</u> God will put them to shame. It will become plain to everyone that they are not true spokesmen for God. <u>They will no longer pretend to have a word from God.</u> All that is left for them to do is to *cover their lips*. <u>They will have no answer from God.</u> Speaking for God has been their business, their profession, but it will be clear that he doesn't even answer them when they call.

God's witness through a qualified leader (3:8)

Micah stands in stark contrast to these false leaders. He declares what a **true** spokesman for God looks like. People need to know the difference between a true prophet and a false one, someone who brings the Word of God and someone who does not.

- <u>He operates in God's power, not his own</u> (3:8a).
- <u>He ministers with the Spirit of the Lord</u> (3:8b).
  He is filled with power, because he is filled with the Spirit of the Lord.
- <u>He represents justice and authority</u> (3:8c).
  He exalts what is right according to the Word of God and condemns what is wrong according to the Word of God.
- <u>He declares the nation's sins</u> (3:8d).
  His preaching is not always cheerful. He is courageous. Though the false prophets are rising up to condemn him, the Lord has filled this prophet with the courage to stand in the face of that opposition and to

preach the truth. His role is to declare to Jacob his transgression, to declare to Israel his sin. That is mercy from God. When a people is living in sin and on the brink of disaster, it is mercy that God would send a messenger to say to that people, "You are on the brink of disaster." Through Micah and Isaiah, the Lord worked repentance and granted revival, and the southern kingdom went on for over 100 years. So, thank God for a true man of God whom the Lord sent to this people to declare their transgressions to them.

God's witness of the devastation to come (3:9-12)

We now see God's witness of the devastation to come. It will be delayed, but it will come when the Babylonians take Judah away into exile. Having addressed the rulers and the religious leaders separately, He briefly describes their sins and just retribution. God, through Micah, summarizes His case and announces His verdict in verses 9-12.

The summary of the evidence (3:9-11)

Its heads pervert justice (3:9). They *detest justice*. They ought to love what is right and hate what is evil, but they take what is straight and twist it. We live in a time when all that is straight is being made crooked. May the Lord grant us the ability to see clearly and to speak the truth in love, detesting what is evil and loving what is right.

Its heads prey on people (3:10). They think they're building up, but they're instruments of destruction. They've built with *blood* and *iniquity*. Perhaps they were selling the story that their nation had prospered, but it was not true prosperity. No nation can prosper by embracing evil.

Its heads sell the truth for bribes (3:11a). The judges' decisions are based on who lines their pockets.

Its priests teach for a price (3:11b). They, too, are motivated by money.

Its prophets practice divination for money (3:11c). It's interesting that he keeps using the word *divination*. (3:6, 7, 11.) It's as though he's comparing their messages to those of the pagans. They claim to speak for the Lord, but the oracles they're selling are just darkness, divination for money.

Everyone has a false sense of safety (3:11d). Their attitude is, "Micah, the message you're delivering, it's so inappropriate. Such a lie. The Lord is here. He will bless us. No disaster shall come upon us."

The declaration of the disaster (3:12)

<u>The people will share the fate of their leaders</u> (3:12a). These leaders will have blood on their hands. God will judge both the leaders and those they lead. The people are heading to disaster because of these disastrous leaders.

<u>Jerusalem will be destroyed</u> (3:12b). They will see Zion *plowed*, Jerusalem a pile of *ruins*, the mountain of the Lord's house *wooded*, an overgrown thicket. Everything they built up by their sinful ways will be destroyed. Their disastrous leadership has devastating consequences.

What does this say to our world?

Remember the proverb, *Righteousness exalts a nation, but sin is a reproach to any people* (Prov 14:34). We are salt and God's light in the midst of our society. We may be the last vestiges of a conscience in the culture. When the whole world seems confused about right and wrong, and about blessing and disaster, it can't afford for us to be confused. We must be clear, loving, gentle, but bold and truthful, filled with the power of God and led by the Spirit of God, as we represent what is just and courageous. We must declare to people their sins, so they can repent of them and look to Jesus for forgiveness.

<u>It speaks to our nations.</u> Though it was directed to Jacob and Israel, it still speaks to any land daring to imagine that God will reward evil. He will not.

<u>It speaks to our responsibility as leaders.</u> Where has God entrusted leadership to you? What kind of leader are you—in the home, in the Lord's church, in business, to your friends? Everyone bears their own responsibility, but we don't want blood on our hands. We want to be able to say, as Paul said, "…*I am innocent of the blood of all, for I did not shrink from declaring to you the whole counsel of God*" (Acts 20:26-27). We're not perfect leaders, but we want to be faithful leaders.

<u>It speaks to the blessing found in Jesus Christ.</u> We've seen evil rulers, priests, prophets, and builders discussed. They are faithless, trying to build with blood and with iniquity. In the Lord Jesus Christ, we have something far, far better.

- He is <u>the faithful ruler</u>. He's the perfect King of kings and Lord of Lords.
- He is <u>the faithful priest.</u> He's both the offering and the offerer, the One Who laid down His own life on the cross to pay for all our

sins, and Who now intercedes on our behalf forever with His own merit. Through Him, we are now right with God.

- He is the faithful prophet. He is the Word of God Himself. In Jesus Christ we find truth and know wisdom from God.
- He is the faithful builder. He has built our lives, and He's building us together as a dwelling place for God. He builds His church and the gates of hell will not prevail against it.

In a world full of corruption, lies, and distortion, we have the Lord Jesus Christ. Jesus is our life and our hope. He sends us out into this world to declare the truth of who He is. The Lord Jesus spoke to Simon and Andrew as they were fishing. He said, "*Follow me, and I will make you fishers of men*" (Matt. 4:19). *Fishers of men* means you go after them. If you follow Jesus, He will teach you and make you into fishers of men. That's why we gather for edification and leave to evangelize the world.

In a world on its way to disaster, God has chosen that we should be His mouthpieces. We are to tell of the disaster toward which it is heading. We are to tell of the good news that you can flee from God's wrath by fleeing to His Son, finding forgiveness of all your sins. Who will tell that to the world, if not us? If not the fishers of men? Remember who you are. Follow Jesus, and He will make you fishers of men.

7
MANKIND'S ONLY TRUE HOPE
(4:1-5)

God has left man, even in his <u>sinful</u> condition, with reminders of his <u>original</u> condition. He has left evidence in man himself, that man once existed <u>without</u> sin and <u>with</u> the satisfaction that was originally given by his Creator. God has put eternity in man's heart, a sense of a larger purpose for his existence. That's what Ecclesiastes 3:11 says:

He has made everything beautiful in its time… He has also has put eternity into man's heart, yet so that he cannot find out what God has done from beginning to end.

Because of man's fall, the realization of that larger purpose and the satisfaction of heart that is found in that awareness is always missing.

The evidences are there in man's desires, but they have been perverted by sin. His desires are perverted in two ways: **what he wants** is now twisted and so is **where he thinks he can find** what he wants. He is characterized by twisted dreams and misplaced confidences.

He desires something that is <u>related</u> to what God gives, but it is a <u>perversion</u> of what God gives. His desires give evidence of something he forfeited by his sinning. He strives for satisfaction of heart, and yet he can never achieve it. He says along with the preacher:

Ecclesiastes 1:14 *I have seen everything under the sun, and behold, all is vanity and a striving after the wind.*

Man wants <u>peace</u>, but without a remedy for what destroys peace, and that is sin. He wants <u>prosperity</u>, but without reference to the true riches, those that are eternal in nature. He wants a prosperity that belongs to the here and the now. He wants <u>unity</u>, but a unity not associated with reconciliation with God in Jesus Christ. He wants a unity that doesn't require forgiveness of his sins. He wants <u>wisdom</u>, but not a wisdom that listens to God and submits to the Word of God. He wants <u>a central organizing principle for his life</u>, something that makes sense of his existence. He organizes his life around all sorts of things—money or family or pleasures—but he doesn't want to center his life on the <u>true</u> center, the God of the Bible.

He is always searching, always trying, always hoping and <u>always</u> empty. When Christ saved us, He both satisfied our hearts and created new longings in our hearts. We long for what <u>God has promised</u> to give and what we know <u>God alone is able</u> to give. We are thankful for what He has already given us in the present, but we long for what He has promised in the future.

Micah has declared God's judgment upon the leaders of the people. He now declares the hope of the godly.

FIVE DESIRES FULFILLED IN OUR ONE HOPE (4:1-5)

With each of these desires there is a total reversal of the judgment. Jerusalem will be razed, but that will not the final end. God has a future for Jerusalem.

The time indicators in this larger section indicate that Micah is talking about the end of the age. He is looking to the time when Messiah will be on the earth. He's referring to the kingdom that cannot exist until the King returns to the earth. This will be *in the latter days* (4:1). It will last *forever and ever* (4:5). It will be *in that day* (4:6). It will be true *forevermore* (4:7). He looks into the distant future and sees something that the Lord God Himself will bring into existence; something that the Lord God will cause to last.

The Lord gives a similar word through Micah's contemporary, the prophet Isaiah.

Isaiah 2:1 *The word that Isaiah the son of Amoz saw concerning Judah and Jerusalem.*

2 It shall come to pass in the latter days
    that the mountain of the house of the LORD
shall be established as the highest of the mountains,
    and shall be lifted up above the hills;
and all the nations shall flow to it,
3   and many peoples shall come, and say:
"Come, let us go up to the mountain of the LORD,

to the house of the God of Jacob,
that he may teach us his ways
    and that we may walk in his paths."
For out of Zion shall go forth the law,
    and the word of the LORD from Jerusalem.
⁴ He shall judge between the nations,
    and shall decide disputes for many peoples;
and they shall beat their swords into plowshares,
    and their spears into pruning hooks;
nation shall not lift up sword against nation,
    neither shall they learn war anymore.

What's described here is an intermediate Kingdom, the thousand-year millennial reign that will be ushered in with the second advent of Christ. We see this kind of reversal in our own individual experience. Salvation produces lives that find their satisfaction in God. We have gone from empty, restless people, to a people who have found their rest in God. As Augustine wrote in his *Confessions*, "Thou awakest us to the light in Thy praise, for Thou madest us for Thyself and our heart is restless until it repose in Thee."[11]

It is God who has taught us to find our rest in Him, but we live in a world that doesn't know that rest. God-centered believers are living in a man-centered world. **Sin** makes for a man-centered, self-centered, temporarily-driven existence, not revolving around God or finding its meaning in God. It puts anything and everything else at the center. The day is coming when the whole world will be God-centered.

A God-Centered World (4:1-2a).

The exaltation of the mountain of the Lord speaks both of its prominence in the minds of people, in terms of its focus in the world, and a physical exaltation. The Bible speaks of topographical changes that will take place at the time of Christ's return to earth. The Lord tells us of a day when the entire world will center on the place from which Jesus will rule.

Zechariah 8:3 *Thus says the LORD: I have returned to Zion and will dwell in the midst of Jerusalem, and Jerusalem shall be called the faithful city, and the mountain of the LORD of hosts, the holy mountain.*

---

[11] *The Confessions of Saint Augustine*, translated by Edward Bouverie Pusey, Book 1.1.1.1

Jerusalem will be the focus of the world because **Christ** will be the focus of the world, and He will rule the world from a millennial Jerusalem.

Zech. 14: 7-11 *And there shall be a unique day, which is known to the LORD, neither day nor night, but at evening time there shall be light.*

⁸ On that day living waters shall flow out from Jerusalem, half of them to the eastern sea and half of them to the western sea. It shall continue in summer as in winter.

⁹ And the LORD will be king over all the earth. On that day the LORD will be one and his name one.

¹⁰ The whole land shall be turned into a plain from Geba to Rimmon south of Jerusalem. But Jerusalem shall remain aloft on its site from the Gate of Benjamin to the place of the former gate, to the Corner Gate, and from the Tower of Hananel to the king's winepresses. ¹¹ And it shall be inhabited, for there shall never again be a decree of utter destruction. Jerusalem shall dwell in security.

We long for the world to acknowledge God's preeminence. We long for the world to acknowledge the majesty, the wonder, the beauty and the worth of God's Son. We long for a God-centered existence.

A Truth-Loving World (4:1b-2)

Do we not long for a world that knows the truth, that would love it, love the Word of God and desire it? It is only God who creates a thirst for the truth.

In this vision of the future world, the nations are streaming like a river into the city of Jerusalem, but not for the reasons people stream into cities today. They won't come merely for sightseeing or shopping. They will be flowing into the city because God's law will be going out of the city. They will be coming for the Word of God, taught the truth by Jesus, the Messiah, standing at the head of all instruction. The people have been devoured by priests who did not teach the truth; they taught for money. Now they will be taught by the Chief Shepherd Himself. Notice they don't want to go **just to be taught**, but are **ready to do** what they are taught. They come *"that he may teach us his ways and that we may walk in his paths."*

They want to learn that they might practice, that they might obey. We cannot claim to love the truth if we are not ready to do what God's Word teaches us.

As the Kingdom begins, there are people who will have survived the tribulation period who will go into that Kingdom as believers, but with bodies just like ours. During that Kingdom age, there will be people born who come to faith in Christ, and people will need instruction and teaching.

Here's why people will flow into the city of Jerusalem to hear the Word of the Lord: because Jesus is there <u>in person</u>.

A Justice-Respecting World (4:3a)

In Micah's world, the leaders were perverting justice. They gave judgments based upon their own desire for enrichment. Here, the Lord God is comforting His people and telling them there's a day coming when there will be no injustice. The Lord God Himself will be the Judge on the earth and the earth will reflect His will. He will rule with a rod of iron. As a result, the whole world will reflect justice.

We long for a world in which justice reigns, in which what is truly right is respected as right, and what is truly wrong is rejected as wrong. There is a world coming in which the nations will have their matters settled by the Son of God. He will give His judgments, and the nations will abide by them.

A Peace-Filled World (4:3b)

People desire peace. Even though men's desires are twisted because of sin, those desires still give testimony as to what man was, what he is meant to be and will be in Jesus Christ. The world is anything but peaceful. Mankind longs for a world without war, without the heartbreak and chaos that is all around us. Despite all of the centuries of peace, arms agreements, money paid, and wars fought, the world still has constant conflict.

The only way this world will ever know true peace, is when Jesus Christ returns to the earth, fulfilling His promise to bring peace. The earth will be characterized by unbelievable fruitfulness. Instruments of war will become instruments for farming. There will be no more need for weapons of war.

We long for a world at peace under the Lordship of Jesus Christ, a world at peace with itself because it's at peace with God. This is the only way to peace in any realm, whether it's in your marriage, in your home with your children, in friendships or in the church. The only way we know peace is because we have peace <u>with</u> God and therefore, the peace <u>of</u> God, and we're able to live lives that accord with that peace. We are peacemakers who make peace not through compromise, but through the gospel of Jesus Christ.

A Prosperity-Filled World (4:4)

The peace—the well-being—that will be known among nations extends to the individual level. Not only will there be peace (no one to fear), but there will be true prosperity.

In Micah's time, houses, lands and inheritances were being stolen by the wealthy. The day is coming when the very One who gave them the land will assure them enjoyment of their inheritance. You notice each man *under his vine and under his fig tree*. There's a divinely-granted satisfaction of heart, so that the covetousness that characterizes Micah's age is missing. Now there's contentment from God as each person enjoys what the Lord has given him. Micah is recalling images of the prosperity under the rule of Solomon, when Israel had its greatest peace and prosperity.

1 Kings 4:25 *And Judah and Israel lived in safety, from Dan even to Beersheba, every man under his vine and under his fig tree, all the days of Solomon.*

Yet we know that this final day spoken of by Micah will be even greater than Solomon's day. This is the personal peace and prosperity ushered in by the Son of God. These are the desires of our hearts granted by God through salvation:

- A God-centered world
- A Truth-loving world
- A Justice-respecting world
- A Peace-filled world
- A Prosperity-filled world

This amazing day will come when Jesus comes. The things this broken world strives for are perverted versions of what Jesus will truly bring, what no one else can ever produce. Jesus alone can produce such a world, and He will.

One Resolution Motivated by the Faithfulness of God (4:5)

Here's a resolution that we can hold onto, because of God's faithfulness:

⁵For all the peoples walk each in the name of its god,
but we will walk in the name of the Lord our God forever and ever.

Joshua declared something very similar.

Joshua 24:15 *And if it is evil in your eyes to serve the LORD, choose this day whom you will serve, whether the gods your fathers served in the region beyond the River, or the* *gods of the Amorites in whose land you dwell. But as for me and my house, we will serve the LORD.*

Micah says in effect, "Let the nations do as they will do." We <u>know</u> what they will do. They will walk in the names of their false gods. Some of those gods claim to be official deities. Some don't, but they are all false gods, and men don't even know they're false gods. People foolishly devote their lives to those gods. They spend hours, days and years in the service of things that have no lasting existence. They give precious time away to things that will ultimately burn, gods that are no gods.

Micah's commitment is <u>our</u> commitment both now and forever. We will walk in the name of the Lord. This is the one resolution we <u>must embrace</u> in light of the future that we know is coming. It's coming because God signed His name to it. He has spoken it. He will do it.

Closing Thoughts

<u>Jesus came the first time to save the world</u>. He lived a sinless life, died on a cross to deliver us from our sins, and He's been raised from the dead.

<u>Jesus is returning to judge the world and to rule it</u>. He's ascended into heaven, and when He comes again, He's coming into the world to judge it. When He arrives, the nations will be judged, and through that judgment, His people will be saved, ushering in this glorious age. He **will** do it.[12]

You're reading this commentary, but what is your relationship to Jesus? Is He your hope? Is He your future? Examine yourself. Are you walking in His name now? Will you be walking in His name forever? If this is <u>your</u> resolution, then walk in His name even while the nations walk in the names of their false gods. "I will live for Christ. *For to me, to live is Christ, and to die is gain,*[13] because my hope is not in this world. My hope is coming. My hope is in Jesus." Is that <u>your</u> confession, <u>your</u> life, <u>your</u> commitment? **Fix your eyes upon Him!**

---

[12] See John 12:44-48
[13] See Philippians 1:21

8
HOW WE GET THERE
(4:6-13)

We can compare what we saw in 4:1-5 to the framing of a house. You frame a house, and then you begin to fill in the details. The outline of the structure—what happens when the Messiah rules and reigns—is in those five verses. Now, in 4:6-13, some of the details begin to be filled in.

Micah has told God's people what is coming at the end, but now the Lord is giving them insight into how they will arrive there. God is graciously preparing them for some of the details that must come before the Lord returns.

We saw that the future of the world includes a time of worldwide peace under the rule of the Lord Jesus Christ. But how will Israel arrive there? Here the Lord gives them information about things near and far: What will happen soon, and what will happen at the end.

THE LORD WILL REGATHER HIS PEOPLE (4:6-7)

They have been *lame*, but He will *assemble* them. They have been *driven away*. **They have been *afflicted* by God Himself,** but He will *gather* them. He will restore them and rule over them.

His Role

The Lord's role here reveals His character. What God does with Israel is more about God than about Israel, just as what God has done with us is more about God than about us. It displays His character and faithfulness.

He treats them as a flock – He will shepherd them. The people are described as *lame*, as you'd describe wounded sheep. He will gather them in such a way that Jerusalem will be a safe place for the flock (4:8). The king who will be in her midst is the Good Shepherd, the Great Shepherd of the sheep.

Notice his promise that there will be a *remnant.* The remnant of what? Of Israel. God will fulfill His promises concerning the nation of Israel in a way that involves the salvation of individual sinners. There will be a believing Israel.

This is not to say that every single Israelite will be saved any more than it was to say that in Paul's day every single Israelite had rejected Jesus. The church in its very beginnings was a Jewish church, but the bulk of the nation rejected its Messiah. In these days, there will be a believing Israel. He'll make them a remnant.

He treats them as a nation – He will rule over them. He speaks of this remnant becoming *a strong nation.* They'll be a people with a dominion and a people with a ruler.

Their Messiah is not only a great shepherd. He is the promised one who will sit on the throne of David forever. He is a great King who will rule over them.

He treats them as a restored people – He is their savior and healer. HE is the one who makes this reality. All of this depends on Yahweh for its fulfillment. He is the one who *afflicted* them. God has punished them for their sins but has now had mercy upon them.

The Results

Because of who God is, and because of what He has determined to do, what will the people experience? What will we see Him do in the lives of His chosen people?

- **SALVATION.** He will *MAKE* them a *remnant*. They would not be one without Him, but He will make it a reality. He will pour out salvation.
- **STRENGTH.** He will make an outcast people into a *strong* people. They will be mighty and numerous.
- **SECURITY.** His rule over them will be an everlasting rule. Though their nation has been unfaithful from the beginning, a day is coming when they will be faithful. They will not apostatize again.

THE LORD WILL RESTORE ZION'S DOMINION (4:8)

He describes the city as a safe place for the sheep. He describes it as a *tower of the flock*, a place where a shepherd would oversee a flock. This is **what Jerusalem will be.**

The *hill of the daughter of Zion* refers to Jerusalem itself.

David Clark and Norm Mundhenk – "The phrase "hill of the daughter of Zion" (rsv) means simply *Jerusalem* and is translated as such in tev. The "hill" is in Hebrew *oPhel* (as in jb), which refers particularly to the area of Jerusalem just south of the Temple, the district where the king lived. Here it stands for Jerusalem as a whole, which is very appropriate in a setting which speaks about the restoration of the city's royal status."[14]

He talks about the *former dominion*. Remember, in Micah's day, the kingdom has been divided. The northern kingdom is right on the precipice of disaster at the hands of the Assyrians. The southern kingdom is being threatened by the Assyrians. This is not a time of great glory. But he says the former dominion will be restored. The day is coming when Israel will not be the tail. It will stand at the head of the nations. His people in Jerusalem will dwell in safety.

The *daughter of Jerusalem* refers to the city and its inhabitants.

The Spirit of God, through Micah, is picturing Jerusalem as a *tower* where God's flock is cared for and watched over, where a king has been provided by God, where its dominion has been restored, harkening back to its glorious days under Davidic rule.

This is a promise of the rule and reign of Messiah.

---

[14] David J. Clark and Norm Mundhenk, *A Translator's Handbook on the Book of Micah*, UBS Handbook Series (London; New York: United Bible Societies, 1982), 197.

THE LORD WILL RESCUE ISRAEL FROM EXILE (4:9-10)

Now, why will Yahweh need to regather a people, and why will Jerusalem's dominion need to be restored? Because judgment is coming before there is salvation. In fact, the Lord's saving work will be on display through the judgment.

Micah Sees a Time of Great Loss (4:9-10a)

There is **GRIEF** (4:9a). They will *cry aloud*. There is **NO KING** (4:9b). Israel will have to see that no merely human king can be her deliverer. She must look to the divine king for deliverance. There is **NO COUNSELOR** (4:9c). The Lord will leave her in a place where she can recognize that wise counselors and sound guidance come from God. There is **GREAT PAIN** (4:9d-10a). He doesn't say to stop grieving. He doesn't say their trouble isn't real. He tells them to *writhe and groan…like a woman in labor*. Is Micah lacking in compassion? Other prophets (except Isaiah) said he was preaching things he ought not preach; they said he was declaring things that would not really come to pass. Remember, their god is full of mercy and compassion with no judgment for them. God was giving a very uncomfortable truth through Micah.

We don't need teaching (or prophecy) that just makes us feel good. We need the truth. So, the Lord is telling them of the pain ahead. He is very specific and says something surprising to the people. He says they are going to Babylon. Now, it is possible that Babylon here is a generic reference to paganism, idolatry, and rebellion against God, making use of Babel from Genesis 11, but God has no problem announcing the future.

Why does he mention the king and the counselor? Because these tend to be the places where people look when they're in danger. Micah is preaching in dark times. The nation is sick with sin. There are threats all around, and the Lord is warning of judgment. When people see signs of danger, where do they look? They tend to lean on the arm of the flesh instead of looking to the Lord.

Today's dark times can be discouraging to the godly. There can be the tendency to think, "O, that the Lord would send us that one leader who would lead us out of all of this! O, that someone would listen to the one counselor who would deliver us from all that we're facing right now!"

The answer is not found in men. It is found in the living God. This is where our nations need to look. This is where Israel needed to look. They needed to look to God and to the One who was promised to them, to their true King, their true Counselor. Here is their true hope, and ours:

Isaiah 9:6 *For to us a child is born, to us a son is given; and the government shall be upon his shoulder, and his name shall be called Wonderful Counselor, Mighty God, Everlasting Father, Prince of Peace.*

Micah is preparing them for the day of pain that is on its way. Right now, the threat is Assyria, but He looks beyond the Assyrian danger and says, *You shall go to Babylon.* That's exactly what happened. As we've already seen, Sennacherib and his Assyrian army come against the southern kingdom, against the city of Jerusalem. The Lord puts a hook in Sennacherib's nose, turns him, and takes them back the way they had come. In the southern kingdom, there's repentance, revival, deliverance. But eventually, the southern kingdom falls—to the Babylonians.

Micah Sees a Time of Great Salvation (4:10b)

Yahweh will redeem His people from the hand of their enemies. *There*—in Babylon, where they'll be exiled—*there* they shall be *rescued* and *redeemed* by the Lord. In 583 BC, the Persian King, Cyrus issues a decree that allows God's people to return to their land, and Cyrus gives help in the rebuilding of the House of God.

Ezra 1:2-4 *Thus says Cyrus king of Persia: The LORD, the God of heaven, has given me all the kingdoms of the earth, and he has charged me to build him a house at Jerusalem, which is in Judah. Whoever is among you of all his people, may his God be with him, and let him go up to Jerusalem, which is in Judah, and rebuild the house of the LORD, the God of Israel—he is the God who is in Jerusalem. And let each survivor, in whatever place he sojourns, be assisted by the men of his place with silver and gold, with goods and with beasts, besides freewill offerings for the house of God that is in Jerusalem.*

It's miraculous that the Lord would move upon the heart of a pagan king in such a way that this is the result. Who directs the affairs of men? Who raises up and puts down? The living God. Only He knows the end from the beginning, and therefore can declare the end from the beginning.

RESCUE FROM END-TIME DESTRUCTION (4:11-13)

Now he looks beyond the deliverance from Babylon to the end of the age. The Babylonian deliverance is just a foretaste of what God will do at the end of the age. The Jewish people realized that. When they went home from Babylon, they understood that this does not compare even to what was, much less to what God has promised for the future. Post-exile prophets still speak of the Kingdom that is to come.

These verses describe something greater—a greater crisis, a greater deliverance. *Now*—The word "now" marks the oracles within this larger message. See it in 4:9, in 4:11, and in 5:1.

God Will Frustrate the Nations' Desire for Israel's Destruction (4:11)

This envisions a future time when the whole world will surround Jerusalem and look upon her, delighting in thoughts of her destruction. In many ways, the eyes of the world still focus on this little land. Some people don't believe God has any plan for ethnic Israel. They don't see the signs. Yet we see glimpses of this prophecy today. The hatred for Jews, and for the nation of Israel, is palpable. Many nations would like to wipe Israel off the face of the map. But God preserves that people, and He will preserve them in the end. He will frustrate the desires of the nations for the destruction of Jerusalem and of Israel.

God Will Punish the Peoples Who Have Gathered Against Israel (4:12-13a)

They have a plan, but they *do not understand* that their rebellious plan is simply a part of God's plan. *He has gathered them.* This world may seem like it's out of control, but it is marching according to the everlasting decrees of our Father. They think they are gathering to destroy Israel, but war becomes a time of harvest, and the harvest is one of judgment upon them.

Rev 14:14-20 *Then I looked, and behold, a white cloud, and seated on the cloud one like a son of man, with a golden crown on his head, and a sharp sickle in his hand. [15] And another angel came out of the temple, calling with a loud voice to him who sat on the cloud, "Put in your sickle, and reap, for the hour to reap has come, for the harvest of the earth is fully ripe." [16] So he who sat on the cloud swung his sickle across the earth, and the earth was reaped.*

[17] Then another angel came out of the temple in heaven, and he too had a sharp sickle. [18] And another angel came out from the altar, the angel who has authority over the fire, and he called with a loud voice to the one who had the sharp sickle, "Put in your sickle and gather the clusters from the vine of the earth, for its grapes are ripe." [19] So the angel swung his sickle across the earth and gathered the grape harvest of the earth and threw it into the great winepress of the wrath of God. [20] And the winepress was trodden outside the city, and blood flowed from the winepress, as high as a horse's bridle, for 1,600 stadia.

God Will Plunder the Wealth of the Peoples Who Have Gathered Against Israel (4:13b)

We see glimpses of God's power in these areas along the way. We see the Assyrians turned back from Jerusalem's gates and 185,000 killed in 702 B.C. (2 Kings 19:35).

But the Bible tells us of something even greater. This looks beyond anything that has happened to this point in human history. This looks to a time when Israel will be scattered during the tribulation period. Christ will go out to war on behalf of a people on the very brink of destruction. He will deliver them. He will regather His people. The whole earth and all that is in it, will be submitted to Israel's King.

Matthew 24:15-31 *"So when you see the abomination of desolation spoken of by the prophet Daniel, standing in the holy place (let the reader understand), 16 then let those who are in Judea flee to the mountains. 17 Let the one who is on the housetop not go down to take what is in his house, 18 and let the one who is in the field not turn back to take his cloak. 19 And alas for women who are pregnant and for those who are nursing infants in those days! 20 Pray that your flight may not be in winter or on a Sabbath. 21 For then there will be great tribulation, such as has not been from the beginning of the world until now, no, and never will be. 22 And if those days had not been cut short, no human being would be saved. But for the sake of the elect those days will be cut short. 23 Then if anyone says to you, 'Look, here is the Christ!' or 'There he is!' do not believe it. 24 For false christs and false prophets will arise and perform great signs and wonders, so as to lead astray, if possible, even the elect. 25 See, I have told you beforehand. 26 So, if they say to you, 'Look, he is in the wilderness,' do not go out. If they say, 'Look, he is in the inner rooms,' do not believe it. 27 For as the lightning comes from the east and shines as far as the west, so will be the coming of the Son of Man. 28 Wherever the corpse is, there the vultures will gather.*

29 "Immediately after the tribulation of those days the sun will be darkened, and the moon will not give its light, and the stars will fall from heaven, and the powers of the heavens will be shaken. 30 Then will appear in heaven the sign of the Son of Man, and then all the tribes of the earth will mourn, and they will see the Son of Man coming on the clouds of heaven with power and great glory. 31 And he will send out his angels with a loud trumpet call, and they will gather his elect from the four winds, from one end of heaven to the other."

Revelation 11:11-15 *But after the three and a half days a breath of life from God entered them, and they stood up on their feet, and great fear fell on those who saw them. 12 Then they heard a loud voice from heaven saying to them, "Come up here!" And they went up to heaven in a cloud, and their enemies watched them. 13 And at that hour there was a great earthquake, and a tenth of the city fell. Seven thousand people were killed in* *the earthquake, and the rest were terrified and gave glory to the God of heaven. [14] The second woe has passed; behold, the third woe is soon to come. [15] Then the seventh angel blew his trumpet, and there were loud voices in heaven, saying, "The kingdom of the world has become the kingdom of our Lord and of his Christ, and he shall reign forever and ever."*

For more on this, read Zechariah 14.

Closing Observations

1. <u>Israel's salvation story is our story</u>. God's plan for salvation, poured out upon ethnic Israel, and his plan for that nation, is the outworking of God's sovereign saving grace and God's faithfulness to his own plan.

2. <u>Israel's Savior is our Savior</u>. There is nothing that God will ever do with ethnic Israel that doesn't find its explanation in the finished work of Jesus Christ. In fact, Israel will see this in the day when the Lord pours out salvation upon them.

   Zechariah 12:10 *And I will pour out on the house of David and the inhabitants of Jerusalem a spirit of grace and pleas for mercy, so that, when they look on me, on him whom they have pierced, they shall mourn for him, as one mourns for an only child, and weep bitterly over him, as one weeps over a firstborn.*

3. <u>Israel's future kingdom is our kingdom.</u> We will all dwell together in the millennial kingdom that is coming.

4. <u>Israel's salvation will mean her *future* joy in what we rejoice in *right now.*</u> Israel's temporary hardening has meant riches for the world.

   Romans 11:12-15 *Now if their trespass means riches for the world, and if their failure means riches for the Gentiles, how much more will their full inclusion mean! [13] Now I am speaking to you Gentiles. Inasmuch then as I am an apostle to the Gentiles, I magnify my ministry [14] in order somehow to make my fellow Jews jealous, and thus save some of them. [15] For if their rejection means the reconciliation of the world, what will their acceptance mean but life from the dead?*

5. <u>Israel's hardness and blindness will be overcome by God's grace.</u> There is no one for whom we pray who might not be rescued by that same grace.

9
THE HOPE OF ISRAEL
(5:1-4)

The hope of Israel and the world is the Messiah. God gave promises concerning a coming golden age: a world that is God-centered, truth-loving, and justice-respecting, filled with peace and prosperity. That day is coming, completely wrapped up in and dependent upon a person. That hope is stationed in the living God, and He executes that hope and accomplishes it in His Son. Israel's hope is her Lord.

Jeremiah 17:13 *O LORD, Yahweh, the hope of Israel, all who forsake you shall be put to shame; those who turn away from you shall be written in the earth, for they have forsaken the LORD, the fountain of living water.*

It is significant that when Paul, a believing Jew, is put on trial for preaching the gospel, he makes it plain that he is simply declaring Israel's hope.

Acts 28:20 *For this reason, therefore, I have asked to see you and speak with you, since it is because of the hope of Israel that I am wearing this chain.*

It is not surprising that as the Spirit of God is giving hope to the people of God through these messages of Micah, there is a consistent mention of a coming ruler. Chapter 5 zeroes in on this issue. You might remember that one of the sad realities of the judgment facing Israel is that she will be without a king and without a counselor. God's judgment upon this people will be expressed by how their enemies treat their king. God, through Micah, describes these dark days, but also describes Israel's hope and the world's hope, the promised Deliverer, who is the Messiah.

THE DARK DAY OF KING ZEDEKIAH

Verse 1 describes a day when the public shaming of the Jewish king will be the undeniable, visible expression of the people's own shame. The description can hardly be explained by what happened with Sennacherib's threat during the reign of Hezekiah. Hezekiah was insulted verbally, but the Assyrian siege was not successful. The Assyrians were supernaturally turned back, Hezekiah was not captured, and ultimately Hezekiah's faith in God was vindicated. If anyone was shamed, it was Sennacherib. In this passage, the Spirit of God is pointing forward to the treatment of Judah's king Zedekiah at the hands of the Babylonians.

Micah 4:10 *Writhe and groan, O daughter of Zion,*
like a woman in labor,
for now you shall go out from the city
and dwell in the open country;
you shall go to Babylon.

The Lord, through Micah, says there will be a captivity and an exile. This will occur at the hands of Babylon. The Jewish king will be put to shame in an unmistakable way. The kingdom falls and the city of Jerusalem falls. He flees, then is captured and shamefully treated at the hands of the Babylonians.

2 Kings 24:18-25:7 *Zedekiah was twenty-one years old when he became king, and he reigned eleven years in Jerusalem. His mother's name was Hamutal the daughter of Jeremiah of Libnah. ¹⁹ And he did what was evil in the sight of the LORD, according to all that Jehoiakim had done. ²⁰ For because of the anger of the LORD it came to the point in Jerusalem and Judah that he cast them out from his presence.*
²⁰ And Zedekiah rebelled against the king of Babylon.
²⁵:¹ And in the ninth year of his reign, in the tenth month, on the tenth day of the month, Nebuchadnezzar king of Babylon came with all his army against Jerusalem and laid siege to it. And they built siegeworks all around it. ² So the city was besieged till the eleventh year of King Zedekiah. ³ On the ninth day of the fourth month the famine was so severe in the city that there was no food for the people of the land. ⁴ Then a breach was made in the city, and all the men of war fled by night by the way of the gate between the two walls, by the king's garden, and the Chaldeans were around the city. And they went in the direction of the Arabah. ⁵ But the army of the Chaldeans pursued the king and overtook him in the plains of Jericho, and all his army was scattered from him. ⁶ Then they captured the king and brought him up to the king of Babylon at Riblah, and they passed sentence on him. ⁷ They slaughtered the sons of Zedekiah before his eyes, and put out the eyes of Zedekiah and bound him in chains and took him to Babylon.

It is that treatment of Judah's ruler that is being described. It is the time of Babylon's triumph.

A call to weak arms (5:1a)

The Spirit of God, through Micah, issues a call to arms in verse 1. The call goes out for "raiding bands" (a small gathering of troops) to be called together in the face of an impending threat. This announces the reality of the threat, and the weakened condition of Judah at the time that it happens. At best, they can muster a small amount of forces for their defense.

An announcement of siege (5:1b)

In addition, the Lord is preparing the people for the reality of a military siege in their future. An unnamed enemy—though they have already been told they will be taken to Babylon, Micah 4:10—is envisioned as having laid a *siege* against "*us.*" Micah includes himself, not indicating that he would be alive at the time of the siege, but that it would come against his people.

An announcement of capture and insult (5:1c)

The ruler will be captured and insulted (to strike on the face was a major insult). Though he is the ruler, his role as a judge is highlighted. As the ruler of the people, he oversees the nation's judicial system. He has the highest responsibility to see that the nation functions according to God's law, and that true justice is upheld. He has failed. He has invited the judgment of God, and the nation's judgment will be pictured in his own treatment.

THE PROMISED DAY OF KING JESUS (5:2)

Even though that dark day was coming, it would not be the end of the story. Another King was coming.

You can see how this verse would have been a real encouragement to the people who would live to see the fall of the southern kingdom. It would seem like everything was lost, but all was not lost. No, there's someone who is coming who will ultimately rescue God's people and rule over them. The hope of Israel and of the world is still on His way.

His birthplace is foretold. He will be born in little Bethlehem, a place of no significance on its own—*too little to be among the clans of Judah.* Look back in the Old Testament's lists of fortified cities and major cities. Bethlehem is not there. It's too small for that kind of mention. *God gave great significance to the insignificant* by virtue of His gift of the Messiah to the world.

God does this in all sorts of realms including the realm of personal salvation. He takes what is <u>insignificant</u> and He fills it with <u>significance</u> by virtue of His own gracious gifts, putting His own wisdom and power on display. He takes what seems foolish and weak in the eyes of this world and does mighty things through those seemingly weak means. He has taken our insignificant lives and has done a significant work. A significant deposit resides within us, the Spirit of the living God. Is that not an amazing reality brought about by the **grace** of God?

The Ruler of Israel will come forth from this little-bitty place on the map, and so out of weakness, the Lord will put His strength on display. The very name of "*Bethlehem*" (house of bread) and "*Ephrathah*" (fruitful) send a message, since both hold the promise of what this glorious golden age will usher in, a period of fruitfulness and blessing.

Also, the fact that this great king will not be born in Jerusalem, indicates that God must go back *to the root of David* in giving *this Son of David*, the divine Son of God, who will sit on his throne forever. The Lord took what was insignificant and filled it with significance—so He would do with Messiah.

1 Samuel 16:1 *The Lord said to Samuel, "How long will you grieve over Saul, since I have rejected him from being king over Israel? Fill your horn with oil and go; I will send you to Jesse the Bethlehemite, for I have selected a king for Myself from among his sons."*

1 Samuel 17:12 *Now David was the son of the Ephrathite of Bethlehem in Judah, whose name was Jesse, and he had eight sons. And Jesse was old in the days of Saul, advanced in years among men.*

After David comes to the throne, people would expect that his heirs would be born in Jerusalem. The fact that the Lord is going back to Bethlehem is another indication that judgment is coming. Jerusalem will be lost, the throne will be vacated, and the promised one will come from the same town as David. David was born in Bethlehem, and God determined that the Messiah would not only come from the line of David, but would be born in the city of David.

Jesus was born in Bethlehem.

Luke 2:1 *In those days a decree went out from Caesar Augustus that all the world should be registered. 2 This was the first registration when Quirinius was governor of Syria. 3 And all went to be registered, each to his own town. 4 And Joseph also went up from Galilee, from the town of Nazareth, to Judea, to the city of David, which is called Bethlehem, because he was of the house and lineage of David, 5 to be registered with Mary, his betrothed, who was with child. 6 And while they were there, the time came for* *her to give birth.* *⁷ And she gave birth to her firstborn son and wrapped him in swaddling cloths and laid him in a manger, because there was no place for them in the inn.*

The people expected that Messiah would be born in Bethlehem. They had read Micah and understood what the prophet was saying.

Matthew 2:1-6 *Now after Jesus was born in Bethlehem of Judea in the days of Herod the king, behold, wise men from the east came to Jerusalem, ² saying, "Where is he who has been born king of the Jews? For we saw his star when it rose and have come to worship him." ³ When Herod the king heard this, he was troubled, and all Jerusalem with him; ⁴ and assembling all the chief priests and scribes of the people, he inquired of them where the Christ was to be born. ⁵ They told him, "In Bethlehem of Judea, for so it is written by the prophet:*
⁶ "'And you, O Bethlehem, in the land of Judah, are by no means least among the rulers of Judah; for from you shall come a ruler who will shepherd my people Israel.'"

Even when the people misunderstood where Jesus came from, they knew where Messiah was coming from. Part of this confusion was that some didn't know Jesus was born in Bethlehem.

John 7:37-52 *On the last day of the feast, the great day, Jesus stood up and cried out, "If anyone thirsts, let him come to me and drink. ³⁸ Whoever believes in me, as the Scripture has said, 'Out of his heart will flow rivers of living water.'" ³⁹ Now this he said about the Spirit, whom those who believed in him were to receive, for as yet the Spirit had not been given, because Jesus was not yet glorified.*

⁴⁰ When they heard these words, some of the people said, "This really is the Prophet." ⁴¹ Others said, "This is the Christ." But some said, "Is the Christ to come from Galilee? ⁴² Has not the Scripture said that the Christ comes from the offspring of David, and comes from Bethlehem, the village where David was?" ⁴³ So there was a division among the people over him. ⁴⁴ Some of them wanted to arrest him, but no one laid hands on him.

⁴⁵ The officers then came to the chief priests and Pharisees, who said to them, "Why did you not bring him?" ⁴⁶ The officers answered, "No one ever spoke like this man!" ⁴⁷ The Pharisees answered them, "Have you also been deceived? ⁴⁸ Have any of the authorities or the Pharisees believed in him? ⁴⁹ But this crowd that does not know the law is accursed." ⁵⁰ Nicodemus, who had gone to him before, and who was one of them, said to them, ⁵¹ "Does our law judge a man without first giving him a hearing and learning what he does?" ⁵² They replied, "Are you from Galilee too? Search and see that no prophet arises from Galilee."

Without that decree for that registration, they would not have been in Bethlehem, but there they were. Why? Because God's Son, the Messiah, was to be born in Bethlehem, as foretold many years earlier here in Micah 5:2.

His role is foretold. Yahweh, through Micah, describes what the hope of Israel would be and do.

- <u>He will serve God's purpose</u> (*"for me"*).
  Ultimately, the Messiah is coming to do the will of God. He is coming to fulfill what God wants to put on display about God. God's story regarding the world and its history is a God-centered narrative, not a man-centered narrative.
- <u>He will be sovereign over God's people</u> (*"in Israel"*).
  The Lord will rule and reign in Israel. The One for whom they are looking is their great King. Micah's already spoken of this in 4:6.

> **Daniel 7:13-14** *I saw in the night visions,*
> *and behold, with the clouds of heaven*
> *   there came one like a son of man,*
> *and he came to the Ancient of Days*
> *   and was presented before him.*
> *¹⁴ And to him was given dominion*
> *   and glory and a kingdom,*
> *that all peoples, nations, and languages*
> *   should serve him;*
> *his dominion is an everlasting dominion,*
> *   which shall not pass away,*
> *and his kingdom one*
> *   that shall not be destroyed.*

> **Isaiah 24:21-23** *On that day the LORD will punish*
> *   the host of heaven, in heaven,*
> *   and the kings of the earth, on the earth.*
> *²² They will be gathered together*
> *   as prisoners in a pit;*
> *they will be shut up in a prison,*
> *   and after many days they will be punished.*
> *²³ Then the moon will be confounded*
> *   and the sun ashamed,*
> *for the LORD of hosts reigns*
> *   on Mount Zion and in Jerusalem,*
> *and his glory will be before his elders.*

This great ruler is none other than Mary's son, Jesus, who is the Son of God born in Bethlehem.

Luke 1:30 *And the angel said to her, "Do not be afraid, Mary, for you have found favor with God. ³¹ And behold, you will conceive in your womb and bear a son, and you* *shall call his name Jesus. ³² He will be great and will be called the Son of the Most High. And the Lord God will give to him the throne of his father David, ³³ and he will reign over the house of Jacob forever, and of his kingdom there will be no end."*

So, against the backdrop of the <u>dark</u> day of King Zedekiah is the eternally <u>bright</u> day, the <u>promised</u> day of King Jesus in verse 2. His birthplace and role are foretold. He comes to fulfill the purposes and plans of Almighty God. He comes to rule and reign over Israel and the whole earth.

His origins are identified. They are *from of old, from ancient days.* Both the Old and New Testaments clearly attest to the divine nature of the Messiah. We could understand Micah's statement here either as <u>the fulfillment of the divine purpose</u> or as <u>a proclamation of His divine nature</u>. One would emphasize an eternal <u>plan</u>, the other would emphasize an eternal <u>nature</u>. Regardless, we celebrate God when we celebrate Jesus. We rejoice in God as we rejoice in the Messiah.

Dale Ralph Davis sees it as a reference to the days of David.

"I have used **'from distant days'** to translate 'from days of *'ōlām'*. Once more Micah himself uses this phrase in 7:14, where it refers to the conquest and settlement period (and/or, as some suggest, the days of the empire under David and Solomon). In Amos 9:11 'days of *'ōlām'* refers to the time of David's kingdom; in Isaiah 63:9, 11 it alludes to the Exodus period and the time of Moses' leadership. With 'days of' or 'years of' in front of *'ōlām* the phrase points to some distant historical time(s).

"Where then does this take us? Back to Bethlehem, I believe. This last line of verse 2 (**'his goings forth'**) is actually simply a kind of confirmation or expansion of the previous line (**'from you will come forth ...'**). Many have pointed out the semi-word-play on the verb 'will come forth' and the noun 'goings forth' (both from *yāṣā*). So the messianic ruler will come forth from 'you' (= Bethlehem), and, in fact, his 'roots' (we might say) go back to 'long ago', to 'distant days'—i.e., to Bethlehem days, the days of David."[15]

Walter Kaiser takes the second approach.

"But this Ruler was not a recent creation, for even though He would be born in Bethlehem, He had existed from eternity. When the Hebrew word for *"everlasting,"* *'ōlam,* is used in connection with God, it can only mean

---

[15] Dale Ralph Davis, *A Study Commentary on Micah*, EP Study Commentary (Darlington, England; Carlisle, PA: Evangelical Press, 2010), 103.

"from eternity on" (cf. Pss. 25:6; 90:2). That can be its only meaning here if the Ruler is none other than the Son of God, the Messiah."[16]

This is the <u>wonder</u> of what God is declaring through Micah. He is declaring that <u>He Himself is coming</u> in the person of His Son. God with man—God with us—is the wondrous reality that the world waits for, pointing us back to eternity.

THE DARK DAYS UNTIL THE GLORIOUS DAY (5:3a)

As is often the case in the Old Testament, the first and second advents of Christ are discussed in the same context. *Therefore* (in light of these facts), Israel can expect an intervening time between Zedekiah's day and the day of Messiah. The day in view here is not His birth (which has already been mentioned), but the day of His return to the earth.

"He shall give them up until that time…" Who will *give them up*? The Lord God will give them up. Even this promised Ruler of Israel will give them up *until the time when she who is in labor has given birth*. A turning away from Israel will come until the day of Messiah arrives. Israel is in a state of unbelief. Israel has been *given up* by the Lord, turned over to their unbelieving condition. They have been given over to mistreatment by other nations, a dispersion and a kind of darkness described in verse 1 and the other judgments mentioned previously throughout this book. Up until our own day, most Jewish people do not believe that Jesus is their Messiah. It is a hardening, as Paul describes in Romans 9-11, but it's not permanent. Right now, we are living in the times of the Gentiles.

THE GLORIOUS DAY OF ISRAEL'S BIRTH (5:3b)

The end of verse 3 says, ...*when she who is in labor has given birth*. This is not a reference to Mary giving birth. It's a reference to Israel, personified as a woman as in Micah 4:9-10.

> *Now why do you cry aloud?*
> *Is there no king in you?*
> *Has your counselor perished,*
> *that pain seized you like a woman in labor?*
> *Writhe and groan, O daughter of Zion,*
> *like a woman in labor…*

[16] Walter C. Kaiser and Lloyd J. Ogilvie, *Micah, Nahum, Habakkuk, Zephaniah, Haggai, Zechariah, Malachi*, vol. 23, The Preacher's Commentary Series (Nashville, TN: Thomas Nelson Inc, 1992), 64.

She will be in labor until her time of pain is over, and that time of pain will come to an end when the Messiah arrives. He's talking specifically of exile in Babylon. I would suggest to you that she continues writhing in the labor pains of her rejection until the time comes and a birth occurs.

The last part of verse 3 plus verse 4 describe what happens when that day arrives. This great King is also the great Shepherd, and He stands shepherding His flock. This is the golden age we learned about in chapter 4. Here we see the same pattern we see throughout the Book of Micah.

A re-gathering of the remnant (5:3)—*Then the rest of his brothers shall return.*

A ruler, Jesus (5:4a)—*He shall stand and shepherd his flock…*

His rule reveals God's strength and majesty. Jesus came the first time in weakness, but returns in strength. The first time the mercy of God is so clearly on display, and the second time the might of God is seen. He is strong to protect his flock.

A resulting rest (5:4b)—*And they shall dwell secure.* He shall stand, so they can sit.

> (dwell) 3427. יָשַׁב yashab, *yaw-shab´;* a primitive root; properly, to sit down (specifically as judge. in ambush, in quiet)… [17]

He stands shepherding in the majesty and might of Almighty God; therefore, the people of God are able to dwell and rest in peace. **He will be acknowledged as great throughout the earth, and this explains their safety.**

Israel's hope is wrapped up in a person, the Messiah, and this is the world's hope. The hope that is proclaimed in the gospel is the hope of the Savior. He has come to save sinners from their sins. He is coming again to rule the world. He will usher in a world that centers on God, loves truth, upholds justice, and therefore reflects the peace and prosperity that exists in a world full of righteousness. Is that your hope?

---

[17]Strong's Hebrew and Chaldee Dictionary of the Old Testament.

10
PEACE AND HOLINESS
(5:5-15)

When the glorious day comes, and Jesus returns to the earth and ushers in His Kingdom, giving rest to His people, it will be a day of holiness. The people whom God defends, He purifies. Where there is true peace, there is righteousness.

This is what grace produces and what CHRIST produces. This is only possible because of the perfect holiness and the saving mercy of Jesus Christ. In Christ, righteousness and peace kissed each other. The righteous requirements of the law found their answer in His finished work.

Psalm 85:10 *Steadfast love and faithfulness meet;*
righteousness and peace kiss each other.

Every act of salvation throughout history, whether before the cross or after the cross, can be traced to the cross. Jesus purchased by His own blood a salvation that exists not only in justification—it is a salvation that results in sanctification, in practical, personal holiness.

The work of the Holy Spirit results in a holy life. It is the GOAL and the DESTINY of all those who have been forgiven and justified by Christ Jesus. We are to be conformed to the image of God's Son, Who is holy.

Romans 8:1-4 *There is therefore now no condemnation for those who are in Christ Jesus. ² For the law of the Spirit of life has set you free in Christ Jesus from the law of sin and death. ³ For God has done what the law, weakened by the flesh, could not do. By* *sending his own Son in the likeness of sinful flesh and for sin, he condemned sin in the flesh, 4 in order that the righteous requirement of the law might be fulfilled in us, who walk not according to the flesh but according to the Spirit.*

Romans 14:17 *For the kingdom of God is not a matter of eating and drinking but of righteousness and peace and joy in the Holy Spirit.*

This truth is under assault today. Many people think Christian love and Christian peace mean we should ignore sin and turn a blind eye to the need for obedience.

This is not a modern problem, but a human problem. In the first century, the New Testament addressed that very issue—the perversion and misunderstanding of grace. To deny the purifying power of God's grace is to deny the very purpose for which Jesus died.

Titus 2:11 *For the grace of God has appeared, bringing salvation for all people, 12 training us to renounce ungodliness and worldly passions, and to live self-controlled, upright, and godly lives in the present age, 13 waiting for our blessed hope, the appearing of the glory of our great God and Savior Jesus Christ, 14 who gave himself for us to redeem us from all lawlessness and to purify for himself a people for his own possession who are zealous for good works. 15 Declare these things; exhort and rebuke with all authority. Let no one disregard you.*

Notice that last verse. This is not optional.

Jude 4 *For certain people have crept in unnoticed who long ago were designated for this condemnation, ungodly people, who pervert the grace of our God into sensuality and deny our only Master and Lord, Jesus Christ.*

Many professing Christians today mirror the culture in the way that they insulate themselves. That is, if you begin to press the claims of Scripture (not mere opinions) upon them, they avoid them by crying foul, trying to saddle the believer or the church with an offensive reputation. They may say, "You are legalists," or "You are judgmental." They want the name Christian, but want none of the responsibilities that belong to that name. They are offended if you expect them to actually follow Christ in holy obedience.

Micah 5:5-15 describes the day of the King. It is the day of the Kingdom come to earth. What will that mean for God's people, for redeemed Israel? It will mean both their peace and their holiness. Their deliverance and their complete dedication to God will be evident.

THE PEACE OF ISRAEL (5:5-6)

As Micah is preaching this, the Assyrians are a great threat. Israel is anything but safe. The Lord, through Micah, contrasts the immediate threat with their glorious future. They will have peace, and their peace will be found in their ruler who rescues them.

He shall be their peace

He shall deliver us from the Assyrian when he comes into our land. Assyria is used as to represent all of Israel's enemies. This is not unprecedented. In Ezra 6:22, *Assyria* is used as a synonym for Persia. No longer will an enemy come into their land and enter their palaces without Israel's leaders taking up her defense (vs.5). Her judgment includes the loss of her leaders, but in that day the Lord will have given her abundant leadership. No longer will Israel be inferior to her enemies. Instead, the people of Israel will shepherd those lands, and it will be a day of deliverance and peace.

THE BLESSING OF ISRAEL (5:7-9)

Israel will be made a blessing to the nations. Verses 7 and 8 tell us that the people, *the remnant of Jacob*, will be *like dew from the* LORD. Zechariah describes something similar.

Zechariah 8:23 *"Thus says the* LORD *of hosts: In those days ten men from the nations of every tongue shall take hold of the robe of a Jew, saying, 'Let us go with you, for we have heard that God is with you.'"*

They will represent a refreshing influence (5:7).

The Lord will use them in ways they have never been used before. John Martin commenting on this says,

> After Christ will destroy Israel's enemies the remnant (cf. 2:12; 4:7; 5:8; 7:18) of believing Israelites will be refreshing and influential (like dew and showers) among many peoples. Because the rainy season in Palestine was from October through March, nighttime dew in the other six months helped nourish the crops. As the dew and rain come from God in His timing (they do not wait for man), so God will refresh the nations in His own timing, apart from man's doings.[18]

---

[18] John A. Martin, "Micah," in *The Bible Knowledge Commentary: An Exposition of the Scriptures*, ed. J. F. Walvoord and R. B. Zuck, vol. 1 (Wheaton, IL: Victor Books, 1985), 1487.

THE STRENGTH OF ISRAEL (5:8)

They will be a powerful nation. They will no longer be like a lamb to be devoured. Other nations will fear them as other beasts fear a lion.

THE VICTORY OF ISRAEL (5:9)

God's plan for the people will result in victory. Israel will be defeated in the short term, carried away into captivity, but will in that day be victorious. They will lift up their hands in triumph over their enemies.

THE HOLINESS OF ISRAEL (5:10-15)

Even as God has purposed to do a work on behalf of this people, He has equally purposed to do a work within them. The One who defends and delivers them will also transform them, leading them in a brand-new course. Verses 5-9 describe a reversal of their physical situation. Verses 10-15 describe a reversal of their spiritual situation. Holiness will one day characterize them; the saved will be sanctified. The Lord will change them in four specific ways.

The Lord will take away their self-trust (5:10-11). This is not destruction of the nation; this is freeing them from what they had once trusted in, so that now they trust in Him.

    1.   Not trusting in military might (vs. 10).
The remnant of Israel will no longer trust in their military might, but trust in God instead.

Psalm 20:7 *Some trust in chariots and some in horses, but we trust in the name of the* LORD *our God.*

Zechariah 9:9 *Rejoice greatly, O daughter of Zion!*
    Shout aloud, O daughter of Jerusalem!
Behold, your king is coming to you;
    righteous and having salvation is he,
humble and mounted on a donkey,
    on a colt, the foal of a donkey.
¹⁰ I will cut off the chariot from Ephraim
    and the war horse from Jerusalem;
and the battle bow shall be cut off,
    and he shall speak peace to the nations;
his rule shall be from sea to sea,
    and from the River to the ends of the earth.

<u>The Lord Himself cuts off their former trust.</u> He is the one who will produce this. He will teach them to have confidence in Him, instead of in everything else. God will transform an untrusting nation into a trusting nation.

    2.   <u>Not trusting in strategic defenses (vs. 11).</u>

The same can be said for another kind of self-confidence, and that is the self-confidence expressed in fortifications. Fortified cities and military fortresses will not be the confidence of these people.

Psalm 127:1 *A Song of Ascents. Of Solomon*

> *Unless the* LORD *builds the house,*
>   *those who build it labor in vain.*
> *Unless the* LORD *watches over the city,*
>   *the watchman stays awake in vain.*

Again, <u>the Lord will teach this attitude</u>, this confidence.

That's what the Lord is doing in <u>our</u> lives This is what holiness looks like. It's learning not to trust ourselves, our offensive weaponry, or our defensive fortifications, but to trust humbly in the Lord.

<u>Self-trust</u> is about pride and <u>what you can do for you</u>. <u>God-trust</u> is about humility and <u>what you know only the Lord can do for you</u>. There is no safety if He doesn't grant safety. There is no provision if He doesn't provide. There is no victory unless He goes to war for you. There is no hope unless He's your hope. There is no satisfaction if He doesn't satisfy your heart. Have you learned that? They will learn what it is to trust Him.

The Lord will take away their sorcery-trust (5:12). The people will no longer adopt false, wicked, and forbidden religious practices from the pagan nations surrounding them. Such a pagan worldview rejects what God has revealed about the world. He has revealed truth about the world we <u>can</u> see, and also about the world we <u>cannot</u> see. God has told us that demonic influence is real. He has told us that practices like consulting the dead, are demonic, dangerous, and wicked. When people do not believe God, they believe in all sorts of things that are offensive to Him and that invite His judgment. This was happening in Micah's day. Isaiah spoke and preached about it:

Isaiah 2:6 *For you have rejected your people, the house of Jacob, because they are full of things from the east and of fortune-tellers like the Philistines, and they strike hands with the children of foreigners.*

Isaiah 8:19 *And when they say to you, "Inquire of the mediums and the necromancers who chirp and mutter," should not a people inquire of their God? Should they inquire of the dead on behalf of the living?*

In this day that is coming, the Lord will make His people holy. No longer will their counselors be those who consult the dead and the occult; they will seek the Lord's counsel.

Like Micah, we live in a day of superstitions. Dangerous ideas, teachings and practices are being imported into the life of the church; things that we don't learn from the Word of God. Two examples come to mind.

The Word of Faith movement teaches that your words create reality. That idea is imported from the world of mysticism. I was sitting at lunch with someone. He was joking, but when someone at the table mentioned assassination he said, "I speak against that word of assassination. I don't want to be at the table if we're going to talk about assassination," as if the very mention of the word would now produce it. It is not Christianity, and it is wicked. It dominates in many charismatic circles.

The spiritual warfare movement has the idea that you and I can really understand how the demonic hierarchy works, knowing the organization concerning cities and nations. It says we then can pray, pleading the blood of Jesus and pleading the name of Jesus and tearing down these demonic strongholds that exist over places or perhaps homes. It is mystical self-deception that doesn't come from Scripture.

I remember when I was a child playing in the backyard with plastic swords. There are people in the spiritual warfare movement who think they're wielding a real spiritual weapon. In reality, they're being mocked by the enemy, because in their hand is a weapon that's no weapon. Satan is not intimidated by that. The demons are not influenced by that. It makes no difference whatsoever when you engage in those sorts of incantations that you think are going to produce some sort of spiritual reality. It's not taught in Scripture. It is not the truth, but an empty, deceptive idea that you've taken hold of.

Holiness is ridding yourself of all that and taking God at His word. What is established in their place is what God has spoken and has revealed. The Lord <u>will</u> do this. Where there's peace and deliverance, holiness is seen. The Lord removes Israel's self-confidence and sorcery-confidence, replacing it with confidence in Him.

The Lord will take away their idol making (5:13-14). <u>He will do this by changing the hearts of His people</u>. They will no longer be idolatrous, worshiping gods of their own making. They will worship the real God.

Do you realize that fallen man's mind is an idol factory?[19] The lost human race is constantly devising false gods for their devotion. Currently, Israel is lost and unbelieving. Modern Israel is an idol factory, just as Micah's Israel was—perhaps not physically (exile had a curing effect on that), but the mental idolatry never ceased. The Lord will save, and because of His gracious work, the idols will be removed.

Do you recognize your temptation to do similar things? Maybe you hear the Word of God only in the way you're willing to hear it. Maybe you deal with the living God only in the way you're willing to deal with Him. Mentally, you smooth those sharp edges of truth that call for change in your life so that you can deal with a god who is only a caricature of the true God of the Bible. You have reshaped Him so He's more comfortable to you and doesn't threaten the life you've chosen to live.

Do you realize how *dangerous* that is? Holiness requires submitting your mind, your heart and your will to the God of the Bible. Then change whatever must change, no matter the cost. He is the Lord; you are not. He is God. You have no right to define Him in your own image. You must be conformed to His.

There is an unexpected reference to cities at the end of verse 14. Why? Because the cities, especially Samaria and Jerusalem, have become the centers for idolatry. There will be no more idolatrous cities, because the Lord will take them away.

The Lord will take away their rebellion (5:15). The disobedient nations who rebel against God will be punished. Now it is no longer Israel, but other nations that are in view. Israel will have been made a submissive, humble and obedient people. In verse 15, we see that the Lord takes away their rebellion because He promises that in anger and wrath He will execute vengeance on the nations that did not obey. When the King comes, there will be a great judgment of the earth. The rebellious will meet God's anger and wrath. The remnant of Israel will not face that, because they will have repented, looked in faith to the One who has come to deliver them. He will be their peace (5:5). He will deliver them from their enemies (5:6). They will have looked to Him in faith. This once was a <u>rebellious</u> people, but now will be an <u>obedient</u> people.

---

[19] Calvin, John, *Institutes of the Christian Religion*, 1.11.8

This is what the Lord does when He saves a person. He changes them from a rebellious sinner to a willing disciple, to someone who desires the truth. We meet with a brand-new kind of heartbreak found in our disobedience, because our remaining sinfulness and the flesh, still abides within us. Don't you long for that day when sin will be gone, and all its vestiges completely removed? You long for that day because your heart has been transformed, no longer rebellious, but submissive, longing to obey the Lord.

We see peace, deliverance, and salvation. Wherever you have true peace, there's righteousness. Wherever deliverance has really been wrought by the Lord, a purifying work will follow. Salvation, in the sense of deliverance and justification, will always result in sanctification. As He delivers this people, He will transform them, and it will result in holiness.

An Application

Is God producing holiness in you? You claim to be at peace with God, having been justified by faith in Jesus Christ. That's the truth of Romans 5:1. You claim He has delivered you, taken you from the domain of darkness, transferred you into the Kingdom of His Son. You claim that all your sins have been forgiven, so you belong to this great salvation accomplished by Jesus. That means you claim you are destined for holiness, because God has destined His children for conformity to His own Son.

If all of that is true about you, are you walking in holiness right now? Not perfectly, but progressively and willingly, desiring the Lord to purify your life? Are you putting away your sins, walking in what pleases God? Do you increasingly trust Him instead of yourself? Are you putting away practices that aren't affirmed in Scripture, superstition included? Are you putting away the idols that arise within your own mind and heart? Do you long to submit to Him instead of rebelling? There is the evidence that what you claim is true, for where the Lord has truly delivered people, He is changing them.

76

11
TREMENDOUS SIN—TENDER INDICTMENT
(6:1-8)

In the Bible we meet God and get a new glimpse of Him on every page. It's an inexhaustible treasure. There's always something more to be revealed, something new to learn, or something to speak to your heart in a fresh way. This passage opens a clear vista into God's amazing character. On our journeys through scripture, we may have already learned of God's mercy and kindness in many different places and ways, but the view that emerges from this text is still breathtaking. It's almost hard to believe. The old hymn speaks of "amazing grace." That's what we have in these eight verses.

We see a tremendous sin on the part of God's people, and we see that sin addressed with a very tender indictment. Indictments are seldom tender, but this one is.

THE LORD CONVENES THE COURT (6:1-2)

This is the beginning of the third and final of the major messages that make up the book of Micah. Once again, the language is that of a law proceeding. The Lord convenes the court, the whole earth sits to listen to the case, and through the prosecuting efforts of the Lord through Micah, the people of Israel are called to account. He calls upon the earth itself (*the mountains* and *the hills*) to hear the proceedings—whether as witnesses or as the jury.[20] He's

---

[20] For the idea of the earth witnessing, see Jos 24:27; Hab 2:11 and Luk 19:40.

putting Israel on the stand. The Lord is about to question his people. In this setting, the Lord puts His majesty, authority, and faithfulness on display.

God's authority (6:1a). He is the judge. When He convenes the court—it meets. When he says it's time to listen, Israel must hear. Even mountains and hills obey Him.

God's eternality and sovereignty (6:1b-2). He calls the earth itself to witness the proceedings, because He was there when the world came into existence, and only the earth is old enough to have witnessed all of God's dealings with Israel, generation after generation. You have heard the expression, "If these walls could talk." If the mountains and the hills surrounding the people of Israel could speak, they would testify to the case that God is laying out—that he has been faithful to this people, but they have been faithless.

God's rights over His grace-works (6:2b). He addresses Israel as HIS PEOPLE. This is nothing less than a creation of grace giving account to the one who issued the grace. Israel has experienced God's grace. Their very existence as a people, their redemption, the way God has cared for them, and all his dealings with them are expressions of His grace and mercy. So, it is absolutely right that they are now called upon to account to the One who has demonstrated such grace to them.

Deuteronomy 7:6-11 *For you are a people holy to the LORD your God. The LORD your God has chosen you to be a people for his treasured possession, out of all the peoples who are on the face of the earth. ⁷ It was not because you were more in number than any other people that the LORD set his love on you and chose you, for you were the fewest of all peoples, ⁸ but it is because the LORD loves you and is keeping the oath that he swore to your fathers, that the LORD has brought you out with a mighty hand and redeemed you from the house of slavery, from the hand of Pharaoh king of Egypt. ⁹ Know therefore that the LORD your God is God, the faithful God who keeps covenant and steadfast love with those who love him and keep his commandments, to a thousand generations, ¹⁰ and repays to their face those who hate him, by destroying them. He will not be slack with one who hates him. He will repay him to his face. ¹¹ You shall therefore be careful to do the commandment and the statutes and the rules that I command you today.*

They exist, and they have a relationship with the Lord, not because of something the Lord found in them, but because he chose to love them and to be merciful and faithful to them. He has given them commandments, but those commandments flow from His love and grace.

God will make the case that He has been completely faithful in His dealings with them. This makes their dealings with Him unexplainable and inexcusable.

When he says He will *contend* with Israel, the Hebrew word means "to determine what is right." The Lord will show that the people have been violating the covenant, and that they are in the wrong when examined against the truly righteous standard, which is God's. He will demonstrate what is right. In so doing, He will be vindicated. Both the rightness of God's dealings with them and the wrongness of their dealings with Him will be on display.

Before we go further, let's realize that he can bring us into this courtroom as well. How has God dealt with our sinful world that deserves His wrath? And how has God dealt with you, if you are a believer in Jesus Christ? You have a relationship with God not based on anything that was seen in you or foreseen in you. It's explained not by you, but by God's choice to love you. He regenerated you of His own doing. He granted you repentance and faith in His Son Jesus. He brought you to Himself. Now you have been saved, and you live forever because of His graciousness to you. What has your response been to God in return?

We need to enter this courtroom and listen as the Lord gives testimony concerning His people Israel and then ask, "Are we any different? What is the case against us today?"

THE LORD CALLS FOR ANSWERS (6:3-5)

Now that He has convened the court, the Lord lays out His questions. It is at this very point that I stand amazed. The line of questioning, though pointing clearly to Israel's guilt, does not sound like a heartless prosecutor. I have listened to a few court proceedings. I have yet to hear a prosecutor who seemed friendly—or even heartbroken—toward the defendant. No, this doesn't sound like a prosecutor. This sounds like a father—a Father who has loved them, who has been faithful to them, and now wants them to see the truth about their condition and its causes.

This is still more amazing when we remember that God needs nothing. He is eternal and self-sufficient, not dependent on His creatures. There is only one explanation for this tender pleading: God's mercy.

He pleads with them and for them. He pleads with them, because they need truth, and don't recognize it. They need to see how gracious He has been with them and how guilty they are. The brightness of God's goodness to them makes the darkness of their response stand out.

The people's attitude toward God

Before we hear the substance of the Lord's questions for them, let's look at their attitudes that the questions address.

They have been _wearied._ They are tired of what the Lord wants. They think it's something wearisome.

Dale Ralph Davis – "This verb signifies being worn out or exhausted (Job 16:7; Jer. 12:5) or, with a more emotional tinge, exasperated (Job 4:5; Isa. 7:13). The cognate noun connotes hardship (e.g., Exod. 18:8; Num. 20:14; Neh. 9:32) that wears down; in fact, worship could be such a hardship or 'pain' that priests regarded it as so much 'weariness' or 'tedium' (Mal. 1:13). So Yahweh wants to know how he has worn them out, how he has been such a drag, or proven so boring."[21]

Have we ever thought serving God is boring or tedious or a hardship? Do we ever feel that the means of grace that God has ordained are tedious or a hardship? How do we think about the public worship gathering? Reading God's Word? Serving other believers?

Do we find energy for other things, but have no energy for the things of God? Does God bore us? Are we more eager to spend our time, energy, and resources elsewhere? It's amazing how much money people spend on their pleasures every day, yet they miss finding real joy in opportunities for financial investment in ministry.

What God calls for is not always pleasant. We will have to work, pressing through hardship as we serve God, but it's not tedious, because it's more than worth the pain.

They have forgotten. The Lord's question in verse 3 reveals that they've forgotten the Lord's benefits to them. They are blind to God's amazing grace. When the Lord addresses their attitude, He calls upon them to remember His dealings with them. This points to ingratitude and a total lack of awareness of how blessed they are. There is a complete blindness to the way that things COULD be if they trusted and obeyed, versus how bad things would be, if not for the grace of God.

It is spiritual blindness that makes legitimate worship boring. You can only become bored in response to true worship when you are blind to God's

---

[21] Dale Ralph Davis, _A Study Commentary on Micah_, EP Study Commentary (Darlington, England; Carlisle, PA: Evangelical Press, 2010), 122.

worthiness of your worship. Whenever you encounter legitimate worship, it isn't the worship that is on trial, it is YOU.

John MacArthur, in a sermon entitled "The Troubling Gospel":

If I take you to the Louvre in France and show you the Mona Lisa and you look at the Mona Lisa and say, "Oh, that's lousy art," I say, "My friend, the Mona Lisa is not on trial; you are. That's already been judged to be a masterpiece. You're a crummy art critic." The point is, you pronounced your own sentence. You're not fit to judge art. If I take you to hear one of the great masterpiece symphonies, and we hear one of the great orchestras of the world play one of the greatest symphonies ever written, and the music is just sweeping and moving and powerful, and it's all over with and you say, "It's all right, but I'll take James Brown," I'll say to you, "Listen, friend. That music's not on trial; you are. If you can't read that as glorious music, you don't know what music is. If you make a criticism of music that has been adjudged by time and men to be a masterpiece then the music's not on trial; you are." And let me say this: Jesus isn't on trial anymore either. We know who He is. But you are on trial, and by what you do to and with Jesus Christ, you declare judgment on yourself. You pronounce your own sentence.

They had forgotten *God's saving acts*. That still happens today. It is amazing to see what passes for worship—what crowds come for such things. How can that be? Superficial worshipers look for a superficial experience.

The Lord's dealings with the people

The Lord questions them. He asks whether they can remember what He's done for them. Just as a father reminds an ungrateful child, answering their complaints—their weariness—with reminders of all his goodness toward them, so God does with Israel. Twice He refers to them as *HIS PEOPLE* (vs.3, 5).

The Lord's dealings with them can be described in four ways:

<u>The Lord has preserved them</u> (6:4a). The Lord preserved them in Egypt and then led them out of Egypt, delivering them from slavery. Remember the Exodus. Remember redemption. Remember the sacrifices and how God worked deliverance through death. Those sacrifices pictured the one great sacrifice of the Lord Jesus Christ, the Passover Lamb.

<u>The Lord has provided for them</u> (6:4b). He provided leaders. This, too, was a great gift. He provided Moses to shepherd them, Aaron to be their priest, and Miriam to give leadership to women and leadership in music.

Exodus 15:20-21 *Then Miriam the prophetess, the sister of Aaron, took a tambourine in her hand, and all the women went out after her with tambourines and dancing.* *21 And Miriam sang to them:*

> *"Sing to the Lord, for he has triumphed gloriously;*
> *the horse and his rider he has thrown into the sea."*

If the Lord gave good leaders at the beginning, but the people are now devoid of leadership, do they connect that with their sins? Are they aware that the Lord is disciplining them?

<u>The Lord has protected them</u> (6:5a). He reminds them of the time when their enemy Balak appealed to the prophet Balaam to curse the people of Israel. Instead of allowing them to be cursed, the Lord caused them to be blessed (Numbers 22–24). This was just one of the public and unmistakable manifestations of God's covenant love and faithfulness to His people.

<u>The Lord has preferred his people</u> (6:5b). He has gone before them. *Shittim* was where they camped before crossing the Jordan river, and *Gilgal* was the first place where they arrived on the other side of the Jordan (Joshua 4). He has established them. He has gone to battle on their behalf. He has given them a land, and brought them into the land, and cleared away enemies before them, and established them in their place.

The Lord has dealt with them RIGHTEOUSLY. He, though committed to them only by free grace, HAS KEPT HIS COMMITMENT TO THEM. He has been good to them. This is what they have forgotten. This is why being weary with God is such a great sin. It is comparable to a man who has a faithful and godly wife, who has done him good and not evil all the days of her life. She is the wife of his youth, but he gets tired of her and leaves her for another woman. His adultery is a great sin, and the heinous nature of that sin is magnified by the faithfulness and love of his wife.

Reflect, Christian, on the Lord's saving acts toward you—His goodness toward you, how He has preserved you and provided for you and protected you and shown you undeserved preferences. And are you weary of Him? Have you forgotten all He's done for you?

THE PROPHET CONCEIVES OF SOLUTIONS (vs.6-7)

Micah now does something very powerful. He puts the response of the people who have been indicted into his own mouth. How might God want the people to respond? How do you respond to such a charge, that you have forgotten and disrespected this gracious God?

The question: How do you approach the God who is in the heavens? What kind of worship does He want? Micah explores possible answers.

Does the LORD want costly sacrifices (6:6b)? Micah suggests not just an offering, but a burnt offering. The burnt offering was completely consumed with nothing left for the worshiper. He suggests not just a calf, but a year-old calf.

Leviticus 22:26-27 *And the LORD spoke to Moses, saying, ²⁷ "When an ox or sheep or goat is born, it shall remain seven days with its mother, and from the eighth day on it shall be acceptable as a food offering to the LORD."*

A calf could be sacrificed after seven days. However, a year-old calf is costlier—it's been fed and tended for that year. He suggests not just a year-old calf, but *calves* (plural). This is a very generous offering. Is this what the Lord wants, just costly sacrifices—giving lots of money and time to the church?

Does the LORD want multiplied sacrifices (6:7a)? Micah now uses hyperbole. He suggests sacrifices that are not just valuable, but multiplied.

Thousands of rams? Ten thousand of torrents (seasonal streams) *of oil?* Olive oil accompanied sacrifices, and people tithed on it (Deut 12:17). But now we aren't just talking about costly worship. We are talking about extravagant, exaggerated worship.

Does the LORD want extreme sacrifices (vs.7b)? Now the hyperbole reaches its zenith. What if someone sacrificed something as precious as their own child—is that what God wants? Does He want acts of glaring personal sacrifice that go beyond anything He has prescribed?

Is He the kind of God the pagans envision? There were pagans who DID sacrifice their children in the name of devotion to a god. Those practices even made their way into Israel for a time. Ahaz (2 Kings 16:2-3) and Manasseh (2 Kings 21:6) sacrificed children. Bruce Waltke described sinful man's reasoning this way:

Blinded to God's goodness and character, he reasons within his own depraved frame of reference. He need not change; God must change. He compounds his sin of refusing to repent by suggesting that God, like man, can be bought. His willingness to raise the price does not reflect his generosity but veils a complaint that God demands too much; the reverse side of his bargaining is that he hopes to buy God off as cheaply as possible. What effrontery to such a mighty and gracious God![22]

Many want to put on a display of worship of God through the extravagant and the extreme, instead of simply being faithful. Are you trying to buy God off? Do you think He demands too much? God doesn't want extravagant. He wants repentant. He doesn't want radical. He wants real.

Is the Lord pleased with external activity divorced from personal devotion and obedience? If you ask, "What does He want?" The answer is you. He wants you—heart, mind, body, and soul. All the external activity in the world will never buy God off. He doesn't need what you have. He doesn't even need you, but He loves you. He loves you, so what He demands from you is what you need. You need for you to belong to Him—completely. What God commands is the highest good for man. *You shall love the Lord your God with all your heart, mind, soul, and strength.* And *Love your neighbor as yourself.* Do you realize that this is what's best for you?

THE PROPHET SUPPLIES THE ANSWER (6:8)

What is the Lord after? What will please Him? What will He accept? We don't want to miss the first part of what the Lord says. *"He has told you, O man."* People are often ready to give what God doesn't want as a substitute for what they KNOW God wants. As Bruce Waltke put it, "God doesn't want ritual purity, He wants ethical purity."

We don't have to imagine what God wants. We don't have to invent it. When people ask what God wants, often it's not a matter of not knowing. It's a matter of not being willing to give Him what he wants, so people try to find something else to offer. No, the living God has told them—and us—what He wants.

Practice justice. He wants obedient deeds, not empty words. The perversion of justice must stop. When you lose sight of Who God is, the suffering of

---

[22] Donald J. Wiseman, T. Desmond Alexander, and Bruce K. Waltke, *Obadiah, Jonah and Micah: An Introduction and Commentary*, vol. 26, Tyndale Old Testament Commentaries (Downers Grove, IL: InterVarsity Press, 1988), 213.

people will always follow. *He has told you, O man, what is good.* God brings this down to the individual level, because this is where national revival begins. It is one man or woman at a time, one heart at a time.

Keep covenant. The word *kindness* is that famous word חֶסֶד *ḥesed* meaning kindness, covenant love, or faithfulness. Keep covenant by how you relate to God and to people. Love God and love people with the love that you find in salvation; the love that's poured out in redemption.

Walk humbly before God. Pride is at the root of their problem. Where spiritual eyes are open, there's humility. When we see things as they truly are, our hearts are humbled by the vision. So, in the place of injustice, fear the Lord by adhering to His laws. In the place of unfaithfulness, fear the Lord by remembering covenant. In the place of pride, humble yourself before the Lord and hear Him.

So, it isn't multiplied EFFORT, and it isn't multiplied ACTIVITY that our God desires. It is a heart that is set on Him, submitted to Him, devoted to Him, and responding to Him. This passage is not a repudiation of the ritual laws God had already given—this is a repudiation of the EMPTY, HEARTLESS PRACTICE of those laws and rituals.

Dale Davis put it very well when he said: "He is not looking for frenzied activities, but for a faithful life (cf. 1 Sam. 15:22–23; Isa. 1:10–17)."[23]

FINAL THOUGHTS:

1. The living God takes note of our attitudes toward Him.
2. Our attitudes toward Him are a commentary on our spiritual condition.
3. The remedy for a sick spiritual condition is not greater external effort or multiplied activity.
4. The remedy is heart devotion. This is a matter of repentance and faith. We can seek the Lord for this.
5. That God would address such a tremendous sin with such a tender indictment reminds us that He WANTS a right response from us. He delights in our repentance and in the granting of forgiveness. Let's seek His face for this today.

---

[23] Dale Ralph Davis, *A Study Commentary on Micah*, EP Study Commentary (Darlington, England; Carlisle, PA: Evangelical Press, 2010), 128.

12
A ROAD MAP FOR REPENTANCE
(6:9-16)

This section addresses a tremendously important issue for our time. It highlights a weakness in today's church, the emotionalizing of the Christian walk. It is the tendency to reduce the demands of Scripture to a mere attitude or feeling, and in so doing, to miss the concrete actions that God is demanding of us. In the name of celebrating grace, we may ignore, minimize, or pervert passages of Scripture that call for actions.

There is another approach to the Christian life that is just as unscriptural. The Christian walk can be emptied of its heart. In the name of a faith walk, some people embrace a mechanical approach to Christian living. It becomes nothing more than a set of principles that you check off one by one as you live your life. That's not the Christian life.

In reaction to emotionalism, and in reaction to legalistic approaches to Christian living, some have fallen into the ditch on the either side of the road. When the Bible demands a choice from them, a putting off of sin and a putting on of obedient choices, they don't HEAR those passages in the way that God intends. Sentiment replaces obedience.

This comes to mind because we have just looked at one of the most famous passages in all the book of Micah. It contrasts mere ritual with sincere devotion. It contrasts an approach to God that is merely external, with genuine worship that begins with and flows from the heart. I'm afraid that some people hear that as saying that attitude is more important than action. As the following verses make clear, if you hear in verses 1-8 that God is only concerned with what is happening in your heart, you haven't heard them correctly.

Micah 6:9-16 clearly explains why God's judgment is coming upon the nation, and what must change if they are to be right with God. It puts into concrete language what 6:8 has just addressed. *To do justice, to love kindness and to walk humbly with God*, is more than a heart attitude. It is not LESS than a heart attitude. Where the heart attitude is REAL, it is visible in decisions and in REPENTANCE. There is <u>a change of mind and heart</u> that results in <u>a change of course</u>, a new life. Where God's people have been sinning, He wants them to repent. He describes their sins, laying out a roadmap for where repentance must occur. If they will recognize these sins and turn from them, the Lord will forgive them, receive them and bless them.

REPENTANCE WILL MEAN HEARING AND FEARING THE LORD (6:9).

The Lord is crying out through His messengers. He is sounding an alarm, warning of judgment that is coming. This is mercy. He doesn't owe His people an alarm, but He's giving them one. He is even describing the nations He will use as His *rod* to discipline them. That word could be translated "tribe" as well, but *rod* is probably the right way to understand this. *Hear of the rod and of Him who appointed it.*

He was announcing the same thing through the prophet Isaiah.

Isaiah 10:5 *Ah, Assyria, the rod of My anger;*
the staff in their hands is My fury!

Assyria is only an instrument. The rod has been appointed by God. God Himself is coming against Israel. Micah has been warning about Assyria and, further in the future, about Babylon. It's as if the Lord says, "Now, here is wisdom. It is fearing God. Sound wisdom is fearing God's name. It is REALLY HEARING God's words." We can apply this both negatively and positively.

<u>Negatively</u>, we can say that they will experience the judgment of God because they DON'T FEAR the Lord. They treat God like a toothless lion, as though He makes a lot of noise, but never executes His threats. They treat Him lightly, as if He is not to be held in honor, love, and respect. They <u>disrespect</u> God at every turn, by turning a deaf ear to His words. They neither heed His warnings nor obey His commands.

<u>Positively</u>, we can say what the remedy is. If repentance is to take place, it will begin by treating the words of God with the weightiness they deserve. It will mean listening to God with reverence and respect, knowing that He keeps His word. His threats are not empty. His promises can be trusted. This is the beginning of wisdom; the fear of the Lord.

REPENTANCE WILL MEAN PUTTING AN END TO INJUSTICE (6:10-11).

In these verses, He begins to describe it. At this point the New American Standard gives a more literal translation than the ESV.

Is there yet a man in the wicked house, along with *treasures of wickedness and a short measure* that is *cursed? Can I justify wicked scales and a bag of deceptive weights?"*

To paraphrase, the Lord is saying to the people, "You are asking what the Lord wants from you. All the while, your houses are full of ill-gotten gains, and you continue to defraud people through deceptive business practices." If people really repent, they *change their ways.* They treat people in the ways the Lord commands. They give God's words their proper weight.

Wherever you have been struggling with sin in recent days, will you change your ways? Will you stop appealing to a mere attitude about God, or a mere desire to turn from sin, and take action by putting away your sin? The Lord knows our hearts. He tells us in Jeremiah 17:3 that they are deceitful above everything else and desperately wicked. In fact, He tells us we don't know our own hearts. The true revelation of what is in our hearts is what we say and do. Real repentance stops mistreating people. It takes action to put away sin and to make things right.

Jeremiah 26:13 *Now therefore mend your ways and your deeds, and obey the voice of the LORD your God, and the LORD will relent of the disaster that he has pronounced against you.*

To *obey the voice of the LORD your God* means to change your actions. *Mend your ways and your deeds.*

REPENTANCE WILL MEAN PUTTING AN END TO DECEPTION (6:12).

Wrapped up in this mistreatment of people is dishonesty at every level. Where there is a true change of heart toward the Lord, He will teach the people to hate all forms of lying. They will become those who love truth and want to walk in truth.

Sinful human beings can become desensitized to the importance of truth. Entire societies can treat truth like it doesn't matter anymore. We are living in a time like that. There was a time when the open exposure of lies would have disqualified a person from high office. Now, people aren't bothered by lies, so long as the lies are by their own candidate.

God is never desensitized to lies. He hates them. Look at Proverbs.

Proverbs 6:16-19 *There are six things that the LORD hates, seven that are an abomination to him:* *17* *haughty eyes, a lying tongue, and hands that shed innocent blood,* *18* *a heart that devises wicked plans, feet that make haste to run to evil,* *19* *a false witness who breathes out lies, and one who sows discord among brothers.*

That sounds like the leading politicians in my country. Just review the list—we have people doing each of these. An entire party stands for shedding innocent blood of babies in the womb. Many people are trying to divide in order to advance themselves.

Proverbs 12:19 *Truthful lips endure forever,*
but a lying tongue is but for a moment.

Proverbs 21:6 *The getting of treasures by a lying tongue*
is a fleeting vapor and a snare of death.

Proverbs 26:28 *A lying tongue hates its victims,*
and a flattering mouth works ruin.

Here the Lord makes plain that what is wrong in Israel is more than just the mistreatment of people. It is the utter deception that is wrapped up with it.

When you repent, not only do you stop lying, but you bring sins into the light. You confess them. You no longer hide them. Proverbs 28:13 says, *Whoever conceals his transgressions will not prosper, but he who confesses and forsakes them will obtain mercy.* This is what characterizes saved people.

1 John 1:9 *If we confess our sins, he is faithful and just to forgive us our sins and to cleanse us from all unrighteousness.*

Psalm 32:5 *I acknowledge my sin to you*
and I did not cover my iniquity.
I said, "I will confess my transgression to the LORD,"
and you forgave the iniquity of my sin.

When we walk with God, we reverence Him by listening to Him. Our ways are changed: we stop mistreating people, stop lying, and confess our sins.

REPENTANCE WILL MEAN RECOGNIZING THE SOURCE OF YOUR LEANNESS (6:13-15).

From a <u>negative</u> perspective, this tells why God's judgment is coming upon the people. If we look at this <u>hopefully</u>, it also demonstrates the way to repentance. If the people will turn from these sins, then God will show them mercy. They will connect their sin to the judgments that the Lord is bringing upon them.

The LORD will leave them weak and desolate (6:13). The first part of this verse is literally, "and also I, I will make you sick striking you." The result of this sickness that God strikes them with is that He's making desolate (הַשְׁמֵם hashamem). Through these verses the Lord wants to make very clear that He's the One doing this.

The LORD will give them over to their leanness (6:14-15). This is a picture of no prosperity. They're not satisfied, and they do not prosper. He's describing covenant curses. They will experience what He warned them about centuries earlier.

Deuteronomy 28:30-31, 38-40 *You shall betroth a wife, but another man shall ravish her. You shall build a house, but you shall not dwell in it. You shall plant a vineyard, but you shall not enjoy its fruit. ³¹Your ox shall be slaughtered before your eyes, but you shall not eat any of it. Your donkey shall be seized before your face, but shall not be restored to you. Your sheep shall be given to your enemies, but there shall be no one to help you…³⁸You shall carry much seed into the field and shall gather in little, for the locust shall consume it. ³⁹You shall plant vineyards and dress them, but you shall neither drink of the wine nor gather the grapes, for the worm shall eat them. ⁴⁰You shall have olive trees throughout all your territory, but you shall not anoint yourself with the oil, for your olives shall drop off.*

Earlier chapters described their trouble from human enemies who take them away captive. The trouble in this passage includes that, but also trouble when nature itself stops cooperating. God sends them leanness and devastation because of their sins.

When someone who's been clearly sinning really repents, they look at their empty life, and they connect that emptiness with their disobedience toward God. They turn from that sin. They turn to the only One who can satisfy their soul.

The Lord does allow His faithful children to go through hard times. They may be in great trouble, but spiritually rich. That is totally different from having a life that's empty because of sin.

REPENTANCE WILL MEAN RECOGNIZING THE NATURE OF YOUR THINKING (6:16).

For Israel in Micah's day, repentance means recognizing where their mind and heart have been. By reminding them of *Omri* and *Ahab*, Micah has connected their current sins with their history. Two of the most wicked kings imaginable represent the very kind of wisdom and behavior that now characterizes their lives. They have practically goaded God into punishing them by their continual sinning.

1 Kings 16:25 *Omri did what was evil in the sight of the LORD, and did more evil than all who were before him.*

1 Kings 16:30 *And Ahab the son of Omri did evil in the sight of the LORD, more than all who were before him.*

If they are going to repent, they must see and believe that their actions are positively wicked. If they don't, then the Lord will give them over to destruction. They will bear His reproach and become the objects of scorn.

CLOSING THOUGHTS

What does repentance look like for a lost soul?

a. It means looking to Christ by turning away from the rebellious way of life without Jesus.

b. It means receiving the gospel (the words of God) with the true weightiness of that message and with true fear of the living God.

c. It means turning away from a life of mistreatment of others and lies to others.

d. It means recognizing that your sins have produced the empty life that you know.

e. It means recognizing the true wickedness of a self-centered, sin-driven, life.

Maybe you're a teacher or even a preacher reading this commentary, and you profess to know Jesus, but as you sit reading this, the fruit says you don't know Jesus. Turn from yourself and your sins. Turn to Jesus Christ, God's only Son, the Savior. Trust that He died and rose for sinners. Turn to Him. Be made new.

What does repentance mean for the believer?

It means the same, except now we do so as those who have been delivered by Christ. It means a return to what is true and right. We live a life of repentance every day. We heed God's words. We reverence Him, honor Him, respect Him, love Him, listen to Him, and submit to Him. Wherever we're mistreating people, we change our ways—not just our words. Wherever we've been living in lies, we put away the lies and we tell the truth. Wherever we've been sinning, we bring it out into the open before the Lord. We confess it. We stop looking to the world and to ourselves for satisfaction. We repent, and we look again to Jesus knowing only He can satisfy us.

Repentance means we recognize that wherever our thinking veers from the Word of God, those thoughts are wicked, not benign. We take our counsels from God. This is a lifetime decision, ongoing every day.

Has the Lord been putting His finger on areas of your life where you need repentance? Listen to His word again from verse 9.

> *The voice of the LORD cries to the city—*
> *and it is sound wisdom to fear your name.*

13
THE HEART OF A WATCHMAN
(7:1-7)

Micah gives us a memorable statement at the end of the fourth verse. *The day of your watchmen, of your punishment, has come.* God's prophets, including Micah, served as God's watchmen, declaring His warnings. They were chosen by God to call the people to repentance before His judgments arrived. In ancient cities, a watchman was stationed on a wall and had the responsibility of sounding an alarm if an enemy approached. At times he was stationed in vineyards and fields during harvest time to defend produce from animals and thieves.[24]

Micah is saying in effect, "We've sounded the alarm, but you've not listened." The Spirit of God, through Micah, is now giving a vision of what the day will be like when the watchman's warnings become reality.

We have seen a glimpse of Micah's public ministry. Now we gain insight into his feelings, how he dealt with it all personally and privately. In these verses we see the heart of a watchman.

You and I are called to be God's watchmen, as it were. We're called to declare His words to our generation. Those words are not just words of promise; they're also words of warning. Do we have the right kind of heart as we take God's words into our mouths? Are our minds and hearts prepared to really serve as the messengers that we are, to a world engulfed

---

[24] Chad Brand, Charles Draper, Archie England, et al., eds., "Watchman," *Holman Illustrated Bible Dictionary* (Nashville, TN: Holman Bible Publishers, 2003), 1660.

in darkness and on its way to certain disaster? As we listen to the heart of this prophet, we need to examine our own hearts.

THE DISAPPOINTMENT OF THE WATCHMAN (7:1)

At the very beginning of this passage, we hear the sadness of his heart. Micah compares his sadness and disappointment to that of a gleaner who has no harvest.

God gave laws that required the leftovers, following harvest, to be left for gleaning. The poor could come into the fields and find something there. This is reflective of the compassionate heart of God.

Imagine that you are poor, and you have made your way out to a field hoping to find food. Imagine your disappointment if you find nothing.

Leviticus 19:9 *When you reap the harvest of your land, you shall not reap your field right up to its edge, neither shall you gather the gleanings after your harvest.* [10] *And you shall not strip your vineyard bare, neither shall you gather the fallen grapes of your vineyard. You shall leave them for the poor and for the sojourner: I am the LORD your God.*

Deuteronomy 24:19 *When you reap your harvest in your field and forget a sheaf in the field, you shall not go back to get it. It shall be for the sojourner, the fatherless, and the widow, that the LORD your God may bless you in all the work of your hands.* [20] *When you beat your olive trees, you shall not go over them again. It shall be for the sojourner, the fatherless, and the widow.* [21] *When you gather the grapes of your vineyard, you shall not strip it afterward. It shall be for the sojourner, the fatherless, and the widow.* [22] *You shall remember that you were a slave in the land of Egypt; therefore I command you to do this.*

Deuteronomy 24:19 is instructive. You don't have to feel like you're providing for yourself, going back to gather even the small leftovers. No, the Lord says in effect, "I'll bless your work and take care of you. You be mindful of others. Rejoice in the thought that through you I'll provide for others also." Verse 22 reminds them that the LORD cared for them when they clearly could not care for themselves, so they should care for others.

Micah compares his sadness and disappointment to that lack of food. In fact, the depth of the prophet's sorrow is heard in the opening words, *Woe is me!* This is not the normal word for woe. (This word is used only twice in the OT.) This is not the word that announced judgment. This is just an exclamation of sorrow: "I am undone—torn up—full of sorrow." He sounds like Jeremiah.

Jeremiah 9:1 *Oh that my head were waters, and my eyes a fountain of tears, that I might weep day and night for the slain of the daughter of my people!*

This is the heart God produces in people whom He sends to address the sins of a people. Until someone CARES for sinners, desiring their spiritual well-being and grieving over the spiritual DESTRUCTION sinners will face, they are NOT FIT to take God's words of judgment into their mouths. That's not to say that God has never used a wayward prophet. God has used a donkey. Jonah certainly wasn't full of the right attitude when the Lord used him. The exceptions just prove the rule—to be a faithful watchman of God, you must have a heart filled with love for people and the desire to see them reconciled to God. Sadly, there are many people declaring woe on others who have never declared woe upon themselves. They may speak God's words, but they do not reflect God's Spirit. We have seen very public examples of this, such as those who have picketed funerals. Many others are not nearly as public with their attitudes, but they preach Christ without the heart of Christ. Theirs is the preaching of judgment without the weeping of Christ.

Charles Haddon Spurgeon said this:

> John Bunyan gives the portrait of a man whom God intended to be a guide to Heaven; have you ever noticed how beautiful that portrait is? He has a crown of life over his head, he has the earth beneath his feet, he stands as if he pleaded with men, and he has the Best of Books in his hand. Oh! I would that I were, for one moment, like that pattern preacher; that I could plead with men as John Bunyan describeth. We are all of us ambassadors for Christ, and we are told that, as ambassadors, we are to beseech men as though God besought them by us. How I do love to see a tearful preacher! How I love to see the man who can weep over sinners; whose soul yearns over the ungodly, as if he would, by any means, and by all means, bring them to the Lord Jesus Christ! I cannot understand a man who stands up and delivers a discourse in a cold indifferent manner, as if he cared not for the souls of his hearers. I think the true gospel minister will have a real yearning after souls, something like Rachel when she cried, "Give me children, or else I die;" so will he cry to God, that He may have His elect born, and brought home to Him. And, methinks, every true Christian should be exceedingly earnest in prayer concerning the souls of the ungodly; and when they are so, how

abundantly God blesses them, and how the church prospers! But, beloved, souls may be damned, yet how few of you care about them! Sinners may sink into the gulf of perdition, yet how few tears are shed over them! The whole world may be swept away by a torrent down the precipice of woe, yet how few really cry to God on its behalf! How few men say, "Oh that my head were waters, and mine eyes a fountain of tears, that I might weep day and night for the slain of the daughter of my people!" We do not lament before God the loss of men's souls, as it well becomes Christians to do."[25]

This section takes the form of a personal lament, Micah's sorrow over the condition of his people. Do we weep? The Lord has given each of us a unique personality. It's not necessary to weep physical tears to be someone who weeps in your heart. But are you heartbroken over this world's condition? Is your heart moved to intercede on people's behalf before God in prayer? Do you have the broken heart of a watchman as you share God's words? This is what we see in Micah: the disappointment of a watchman.

THE DESCRIPTION OF THE WOEFUL CONDITIONS (7:2-4a)

Here Micah points out four things about the woeful condition that caused his sorrow.

The absence of godly people (7:2a)

Micah's heart is broken, first of all, by the absence of godly people. He looks at society at large, and what he sees is ungodly. There is a remnant, even in his day. The revival that will follow his preaching demonstrates that. Yet when he is preaching this message, the spiritual condition of his people is at such a low place that it seems to him as if all the godly have perished.

Where are the godly? Where are people whose lives are set apart from the world, people who live according to God's Word, people of integrity who are spiritually strong, yet spiritually warm, and trustworthy? We may look about us and ask—and find only a few. There are sound churches scattered around the world. Times may be dark, but thank God that there are many godly people.

---

[25] C. H. Spurgeon, *C. H. Spurgeon's Autobiography, Compiled from His Diary, Letters, and Records, by His Wife and His Private Secretary, 1834–1854*, vol. 1 (Cincinnati; Chicago; St. Louis: Curts & Jennings, 1898), 329.

The presence of wicked people (7:2b-4)

Instead of seeing godly and upright people, Micah sees his whole nation seemingly engulfed in the darkness of wickedness—murderous, devious, evil, dishonest wickedness. What did Micah see?

<u>Vicious people (7:2b).</u> They hunt for each other. They set traps, waiting to overtake and ensnare each other.

<u>Evil people (7:3a).</u> They work at evil. They seek to excel at it. (The Hebrew reads, "Upon evil are both their hands to do it well.") Instead of being ashamed of evil, they are experts in it.

<u>Corrupt people (7:3b).</u> The ruler (prince) and the judge are looking for bribes. The great man gives voice to what he wants, and what he wants is evil. These people all conspire (weave, twist, or pervert) together. The ruler <u>wants</u> a particular outcome, the judge makes sure that he <u>gets</u> that outcome, and the evil, great people in society <u>direct</u> all of it. They get what they want in the end.

<u>Worthless people (7:4a).</u> The very best of them is no good. Like a brier or a thorn, they are dangerous and useless, good for nothing except to wound. When a godly man looks at his world, he often sees that the godly are almost non-existent. His heart breaks. He's like Lot in Sodom:

2 Peter 2:8 *(… that righteous man lived among them day after day, he was tormenting his righteous soul over their lawless deeds that he saw and heard)*

Do you see vicious, evil leaders around you? Do you see them putting both hands to it shamelessly? If this characterizes most of your nation's leaders, does it break your heart?

Such conditions are significant for any nation, at any time in history. If there is an absence of godliness in our land, we should grieve and should long for increased godliness in it. We should long for the church to be strong in our culture, not only for the eternal wellbeing of souls, but also for the temporal wellbeing of the land we live in.

Proverbs 28:12 *When the righteous triumph, there is great glory,*
but when the wicked rise, people hide themselves.

Proverbs 29:2 *When the righteous increase, the people rejoice,*
but when the wicked rule, the people groan.

1 Timothy 2:1-2 *First of all, then, I urge that supplications, prayers, intercessions, and thanksgivings be made for all people, ² for kings and all who are in high positions, that we may lead a peaceful and quiet life, godly and dignified in every way.*

We're taught in 1 Timothy 2 to pray for our leaders. In the context of that chapter, we're to pray for their salvation. One motivation for that prayer, in addition to wanting their salvation, is our desire for God's people to be able to live in peace. Godly people must be prepared to suffer, and should accept persecution with joy, but people who would not desire a peaceful existence, and open doors to spread the gospel, are foolish.

THE DEGRADATION OF SOCIETY AT ITS FOUNDATIONS (7:4b-6)

Society has now reached a place of almost complete degradation. The day that God's watchmen have been warning about will come. It will be chaotic, full of confusion. Society is coming apart at the seams. The very foundation of the building is crumbling.

No one to save (7:4b). The day of the watchmen has come. Having turned their back on the watchmen's words—God's words, they are left to their own confusion. God in His great grace has been sending messengers to sound the alarms. They have not listened. The day of the punishment has arrived.

No one to trust (7:5). Micah's description turns from society in general, to the relationships that should be closest. When a society hits rock bottom, it becomes each man for himself. A self-centered world does not keep covenants. When that day arrives, and you are without God, there will be no one to put your trust in—not a neighbor, not a friend, not even a spouse.

No one to rely on (7:6). Even natural affection is lost, as the family manifests the breakdown in society due to sin. There is no one to rely on. The closest relationships reveal the sinful heart of man. A man's enemies will be the people in his own family. The Lord is describing the hatefulness, the utter lack of love, of people who reject the true God.

The Lord has released the brakes. He's let the society run deeper and deeper into the darkness of its own sin. Finally, it reaches the place where it knows no love, no loyalty. Even natural affection is gone. The degradation has reached the very foundations of society.

Take an honest assessment of your own world. Do you see the breakdown of society to its very foundations?

As believers, we'll experience rejection by every level of society because of our faith in Christ. Matthew 10:32-40 shows how Jesus applied this truth.

- Where there's genuine salvation, there's acknowledgement of Jesus, and no ultimate denial of Him (:32-33).
- There's enmity, even from members of our own household, because sinners hate God and His people (:34-36).
- We must be prepared to live out our love and loyalty to Jesus Christ (:37).
- We must be willing to give up all we are, for Him (:38-39).
- The way people treat us will really be how they treat Him (:40). What an honor, to be regarded as He is in an unbelieving world!

Will you follow Jesus? If it means you lose every earthly relationship you've ever delighted in, will you follow Him? Will you love Him even more?

Don't forget, <u>bringing the message of God's judgment to His people broke Micah's heart</u>. How do we cope if we're given such a task in a society that's growing ever darker? Within history, there are bright periods of revival, but what if we're in a dark time? How does godly Micah respond to it?

THE DETERMINATION OF THE WATCHMAN (7:7)

Micah is characterized by sorrow, but also by determination. He has already determined something for HIS LIFE. He stands apart from those who stand apart from God.

He will look to God (7:7a). He will fix his eyes on God. He will walk with God. Micah's confidence and hope are in God, not in this world. It's right that we should be sorrowful, but <u>not hopeless</u> and <u>not faithless</u>. If you are becoming hopeless and faithless, you need to redirect your gaze.

He will wait for God (7:7b). He will not live in the kind of fear that might direct him to look somewhere else for his safety and his peace. When he thinks about deliverance from the chaos of his culture, he <u>looks</u> for the day when the Lord will change it all. He will <u>wait</u> for the living God to transform his situation. Micah has his hope in the right place, not only for the next world, but for this world. If you wait for the Lord, you don't take matters into your own hands, relying on things you should never rely on.

You put away fear and replace it with faith. David wrote about this in Psalm 37. Study it to see how he rejected worry and envy and anger, knowing that the waiting is just a little while. He chose to delight himself in the Lord, to do good, to live for the Lord, to make faithfulness his friend. He told himself to delight in the Lord, knowing that He will give him the desires of his heart.

He will rest in God (7:7c). He will direct his prayers to God, and he knows that God will hear him.

Summary

This is the heart of a watchman.

- He loves the people to whom he preaches.
- He grieves over their sinful condition and the wrath toward which they are headed.
- He loves the godly and takes his stand among them, and he mourns the scarcity of those people.
- He sees the world's condition accurately.
- He announces that condition with the hope of repentance.

Whatever comes, he is determined to trust God, to wait on God, and to rest in God, until the Lord's salvation arrives. Are you a watchman?

To know where our hearts should be, remember the greatest Watchman this world has ever known. God spoke to this world in many ways, through many different kinds of people until the day when God spoke to this world in His Son. Jesus said He came into the world not to condemn it, but to save it. He told of wrath that's coming, but He is the Savior. All the Old Testament prophets, including Micah, pointed forward to Him. All the New Testament revelation points back to Him. Today we say to the world, "There is someone who can save the sinner individually, and one day will save the world, and His name is Jesus. Look to Him. Trust in Him. Rest in Him. Wait for Him."

As watchmen, we urge one another and everyone else to trust Jesus, to escape the coming wrath, and to be watchmen who warn others.

14
HOW THE REMNANT RESPONDS
(7:8-10)

Micah 7 not only gives us insight into the heart of a watchman, it also gives insight into the hearts of those who HEED the watchman. They heed the watchman because they heed God's Word. Verses 1-7 present the faithful prophet; verses 8-10 present the faithful people. What is said here, taken as a whole, could not be in the mouths of unbelievers.

Micah is a representative of Israel's believing remnant. He gives voice to their thoughts and feelings concerning the coming judgment. We must not divorce this teaching from our own situation. When a nation—any nation at any time in history—has been presented the truth and then descends into great spiritual darkness, difficult times are ahead.

In addition to the spiritual sorrow of seeing rampant wickedness and seeing people reject the truth he preaches, Micah has the additional sorrow of having to experience the consequences of the people's rejection of God.

Verses 8-10 present the city of Jerusalem, embodied in and represented by a believing remnant. We will look at our verses under three headings.

THE REMNANT AND HER ENEMIES (7:8)

Jerusalem is personified here and expresses what will be true of the remnant.

Verse 8: *Rejoice not over me, O my enemy…*

The Lord is using Assyria and Babylon like a rod in His hand. Ultimately, the people are experiencing the Lord's indignation. If you're a believer living in ANY nation suffering for her sins, you are not exempt from mocking by your nation's enemies. For example, if a nation known in the past for the gospel is conquered by a Muslim land, and Sharia becomes the law, you can be sure that Christians there would be mocked. The question is: how will you respond?

In the case of Israel, a nation that bore the name and the reputation of the Lord, there was a special hatred, a special kind of SPIRITUAL mocking from her enemies.

It is no secret that for as long as Israel has existed there has been a unique hatred for that people throughout the world, and especially in her geographical region. Here in verse 8, the city of Jerusalem is pictured as having fallen. Like a prisoner of war, she sits in darkness. Verse 10 shows that she has been mocked with very familiar words. They are heard every time an enemy has triumphed over Israel. *"Where is the LORD your God?"* People mock: Where is he? Where is his power? Where is his ability to preserve you? The people of Israel are mocked individually and nationally.

Joel 2:17 *Between the vestibule and the altar let the priests, the ministers of the LORD, weep and say, "Spare your people, O LORD, and make not your heritage a reproach, a byword among the nations. Why should they say among the peoples, 'Where is their God?'"*

Psalm 42:3 *My tears have been my food day and night, while they say to me all the day long, "Where is your God?"*

Psalm 79:10 *Why should the nations say, "Where is their God?" Let the avenging of the outpoured blood of your servants be known among the nations before our eyes!*

Psalm 115:2 *Why should the nations say, "Where is their God?"*

If you are a believer living in Micah's day, what do you know about the judgment that Micah has been proclaiming—about the curses that were set forth in the law of Moses? Your current circumstances do not say that the God of the Bible is not real, nor that he is not able to keep you safe. These troubles are the result of sin. Curses are included in the covenant that He made with you, and tell what would happen if you prove to be unfaithful to that covenant. This disaster has really been expected all along. It is precisely what God promised in His word, and then warned about until the Day of the Watchmen arrived! What a picture that was in verse 4!

Micah 7:4b *The day of your watchmen, of your punishment has come; now their confusion is at hand.*

The remnant knows this is not the end (7:8a). The watchmen have been warning, warning, mercifully warning, and the people have refused to listen. Therefore, Jerusalem has fallen and sits in darkness. In the face of mocking, the remnant says Jerusalem will rise again.

The remnant knows that the light is the LORD Himself (7:8b). They will rise—not because of themselves, but because the Lord will be a light to them. Even when they are in darkness, being mocked, there is confidence in the Lord Himself, and even a WARNING to those enemies that this is not the end.

THE REMNANT AND THE LORD'S INDIGNATION (7:9a)

The remarkable words in verse 9 make it certain that what is being expressed in these verses is the mindset of believing people.

The fall and the darkness are due to the Lord (7:9a). Israel's enemies imagine that THEY have conquered Israel. Israel's conquerors, whether the Assyrians or the Babylonians, or any other nation, ascribe victory to their own power, their wisdom, or even their false gods. Not so, says the remnant. It is the Lord who has done this to us. We have provoked Him. It is the Lord's *indignation* that is on display.

The fall and the darkness are due to sin (7:9b). Why is the Lord angry? He's angry because of the people's disobedience. Amazingly, the remnant owns this sin and confesses this sin. *I have sinned against Him.*

Can we say the same? If your nation or mine is experiencing a measure of God's judgment, do we, the church, recognize our part in that sin? If really difficult times come upon our nation, will we trace the cause to the nation's sin, and will the believing church be willing to own our part in it?

As God's people, are we confessing our sins? Have we sinned by not praying? By not evangelizing? By not preaching clearly and faithfully? By not loving one another? Do we find it easier to chide the culture instead of confessing our own sins?

THE REMNANT AND THE LORD'S VINDICATION (7:9b-10)

Consider the remnant's perspective on her future circumstances. Even though the believer suffers right along with an unbelieving world, there's still a clear distinction between those who believe and those who don't. As we've noted, the believer sees God's hand in the circumstances and confesses his own sins to God. The believer also has assurance regarding the future. What does the believing remnant see?

Temporary difficulty (7:9). The first distinction is that the believer knows his suffering for sins is temporal. The Lord has forgiven him and delivered him from his sins, so his (or her) eternal wellbeing is assured. *I will bear the indignation of the Lord,* but not forever, just *until he pleads my cause and executes judgment for me.*

Temporary darkness (7:9). There's darkness now, but the day is coming when *He will bring me out to the light.* The truth will be told eventually. *Light* may refer to both hope and vindication.

Temporary dishonor (7:10). When that day arrives, the enemies of God's people will be put to public shame, and the shamed people of God will be honored. This is the future for God's people and all her enemies. The enemy will see the total change of circumstances. They will be shamed, treated the way they treated God's people. They will be put in the mud, trampled down like mire in the streets.

In summary, here's what we can say about the heart attitude of the believing remnant in a land under God's judgment.

1. They relate to their enemies with faith, confidence and even warning compassion. God enables them to do this.

2. They relate to God's temporal judgment by acknowledging that it is his work and is deserved. In the midst of it, they confess their own sins.

3. They relate to the future, believing God's promises that the current dark times are not forever. They expect light, truth and righteousness to break forth. They expect honor and public vindication.

15
WHO IS A GOD LIKE YOU?
(7:11-20)

Who is a God like You? That's the question that Micah asks in verse 18. It's a rhetorical question. The answer is clear. There is no one like the Lord. Micah posed the question for the purpose of praise. By the grace of God, he has seen the Lord's amazing character, and he wants everyone else to see it, too.

This is the desire of everyone who has ever come to realize Who God really is. If God, by His grace, has shown you Who He is, then you know He's amazing, and you want everyone else to know, too. Your view of God is a test of the genuineness of your salvation.

Micah's very name means "Who is like Yahweh," and as he comes to the end of his prophecy, he drives home the truth that mirrors his name.

Who is like God? He alone is self-existent. He alone is completely independent and self-sufficient. Only God is *Holy, holy, holy*, the standard of holiness. No one is like him in power…in presence…in knowledge. Micah knows that the Lord is unique in a host of ways. Yet when he wants to show God's uniqueness, at the forefront of his mind is God's amazing grace (7:18). There is nothing any more amazing about God than His mercy toward people who deserve His wrath. Who is like this God?

Has God's mercy toward you ever amazed you?

In 7:1-7, Micah has expressed his confidence in the Lord despite God's impending judgment of the nation of Israel. *But as for me, I will look to the Lord; I will wait for the God of my salvation; my God will hear me* (7:7). In 7:8-10, the city of Jerusalem is personified, and the voice of the remnant is heard, and they also proclaim their confidence in the Lord. They acknowledge their sin—*I will bear the indignation of the Lord because I've sinned against Him* (7:9)—and also their confidence in their future—*until he pleads my cause and executes judgment for me. He will bring me out to the light; I shall look upon his vindication.* That's why he could say (7:8)—*Rejoice not over me, O my enemy; when I fall, I shall rise; when I sit in darkness, the Lord will be a light to me.*

7:11-20 tells us why they have reason to hope. They are looking toward the Day. The Day of the Lord is a major concept in the Old Testament. It will be a day of blessing and of judgment, depending on your relationship to God when it arrives.

We now know that we're really talking about the day of Jesus' second coming when He will return to the earth to rule it. It will be a day of great blessing for God's people and a day of judgment for the nations that have rejected the living God. Shining through all that Micah reveals about that day is the Lord's uniqueness, especially in His demonstration of grace.

There are three clear sections in these final verses, each pointing us to the greatness of God: (1) He is a God who keeps His promises (vs.11-13) (2) He is a God who shepherds His people (vs.14-17) (3) He is a God who pardons sinners (vs.18-20).

HE IS A GOD WHO KEEPS HIS PROMISES, 7:11-13

Who is like God? He's absolutely faithful to everything He has ever said.

7:11-13: *A day for the building of your walls!*—"You" is the city of Jerusalem. God made clear promises to His people Israel regarding a land and concerning Jerusalem, its capital city. God made these commitments to Israel for no other reason than that He chose to love them. God's love for Israel is not explained by Israel, but by His free and sovereign grace.

What is envisioned in these verses is the restoration of the fallen city. In verse 8, they confessed that though they've fallen, they will rise; though they're in darkness, the Lord will bring them into the light. Now Micah describes *that day* of resurrection as it were, *that day* of deliverance from darkness into light.

For Jerusalem, it will be

- *A day for building the city's walls.* (7:11a) The word for *walls* is not the high wall of a fortified city, but the kind of wall that would be around a vineyard. She has no need of high, fortified walls. The Lord will be her wall of protection.
- *A day when Jerusalem will be the centerpiece of the nations.* (7:12)

This day will be a worldwide acknowledgment of God and His people. It will come from their immediate enemies, the Assyrians, and from their ancient enemy, Egypt, and will expand to include the whole region, the whole of their world. God's unconditional covenant with Abram promised him an inheritance that included a land.

Genesis 12:1 *Now the LORD said to Abram, "Go from your country and your kindred and your father's house to the land that I will show you. ² And I will make of you a great nation, and I will bless you and make your name great, so that you will be a blessing. ³ I will bless those who bless you, and him who dishonors you I will curse, and in you all the families of the earth shall be blessed."*

That is fulfilled in the Lord Jesus Christ, but the fact that Jesus fulfills it doesn't obliterate the individual elements of those promises. He reiterates this in Genesis 15 when he cuts the covenant with Abram and the Lord Himself alone passes through the pieces of that cut animal to indicate that this is an unconditional promise that God will fulfill by Himself.

As mentioned earlier, there are promises concerning the city of Jerusalem throughout the Old Testament.

Zechariah 2:1 *And I lifted my eyes and saw, and behold, a man with a measuring line in his hand! ² Then I said, "Where are you going?" And he said to me, "To measure Jerusalem, to see what is its width and what is its length." ³ And behold, the angel who talked with me came forward, and another angel came forward to meet him ⁴ and said to him, "Run, say to that young man, 'Jerusalem shall be inhabited as villages without walls, because of the multitude of people and livestock in it. And I will be to her a wall of fire all around, declares the LORD, and I will be the glory in her midst.'"*

In verses 11 and 12, we see that the Lord will keep His word. He is a covenant-keeping God.

- *A day when disobedience will be punished.* (7:13)

When the Lord Jesus returns to the earth, the sheep will be separated from the goats. His people will be brought into the blessing He's promised; those who have continued to reject Him and rebel against Him will be punished. Not everybody will acknowledge the truth in that day. When Jesus returns, there will be the rebellious among the nations. He will separate them out and they will be purged from the earth. Then His Kingdom will begin, with only believers. Isaiah prophesied about that day.

Isaiah 24:1 *Behold, the LORD will empty the earth and make it desolate,*
    and he will twist its surface and scatter its inhabitants.
² And it shall be, as with the people, so with the priest;
    as with the slave, so with his master;
    as with the maid, so with her mistress;
  as with the buyer, so with the seller;
    as with the lender, so with the borrower;
      as with the creditor, so with the debtor.
³ The earth shall be utterly empty and utterly plundered;
  For the LORD has spoken this word.

Great or small, the disobedient will be punished and God's people will be blessed. The Lord is faithful—Sovereign—All-powerful. This is who He is. Who is like Him?

HE IS A GOD WHO SHEPHERDS HIS PEOPLE, 7:14-17

This is not just a day about land and cities. It's a day when God will display His unique, loving relationship with His people. God will demonstrate His ability to produce a believing and faithful ethnic Israel.

This is not a denial of the unity of salvation, nor a denial of the oneness of God's people throughout the ages in terms of salvation. But in my view, some want to take that truth of the unity of salvation and then destroy the individual threads of beautiful color that God has woven throughout His salvation work. They want to flatten it all out and make it all grey.

The Lord will do this saving work in a way that fulfills the various threads of His promise of salvation. He will fulfill His promise to pour out salvation on ethnic Jews. We are living in the times of the Gentiles. The Lord is pouring out salvation upon Gentiles in great numbers. A day will come when there will be an awakening among ethnic Israel. There will be a great outpouring of salvation. As we enter the Kingdom of Jesus Christ, there will be a believing Israel. And He will shepherd all His people, including ethnic Israel. When He does this, it will be an answer to prayers throughout the generations. Micah 7:14 is one of those prayers.

Micah Prays and the Lord Responds (7:14-15). Here, God's people are pictured as being placed by God into a unique relationship with Himself. God has chosen and saved them. Their history throughout the Old Testament is different from the nations.

This is the very description of Israel that Balaam gave when Balak wanted him to curse the people of God. In Numbers 23:9, we read: *For from the top of the crags I see him, from the hills I behold him; behold, a people dwelling alone, and not counting itself among the nations!*

One reason for Balak's hatred for the people of God was the fact that they were distinct. Here in Micah 7:14 they are pictured again dwelling alone in a forest *in the midst of Carmel* (translated "a garden land").

The *rod* or *staff* speaks of **protection**. The grazing speaks of **provision**, so the prayer is, "Lord, shepherd us in a way that protects us and provides for us. We'll know food from Your hand and we'll know fellowship with You. Give Your people safety. Give them sustenance, Lord."

In 7:15, God answers this prayer. He is speaking. He will shepherd them and do miraculous things, causing people to marvel, as He did in the days of the Exodus. He will lead His people out of the places where they have been scattered all over the world and bring them into their land where He will provide for them. It will be as amazing as the Exodus.

Ezekiel 34:11 *"For thus says the Lord GOD: Behold, I, I myself will search for my sheep and will seek them out. 12 As a shepherd seeks out his flock when he is among his sheep that have been scattered, so will I seek out my sheep, and I will rescue them from all places where they have been scattered on a day of clouds and thick darkness. 13 And I will bring them out from the peoples and gather them from the countries, and will bring them into their own land. And I will feed them on the mountains of Israel, by the ravines, and in all the inhabited places of the country. 14 I will feed them with good pasture, and on the mountain heights of Israel shall be their grazing land. There they shall lie down in good grazing land, and on rich pasture they shall feed on the mountains of Israel. 15 I myself will be the shepherd of my sheep, and I myself will make them lie down, declares the Lord GOD. 16 I will seek the lost, and I will bring back the strayed, and I will bind up the injured, and I will strengthen the weak, and the fat and the strong I will destroy. I will feed them in justice.*

It's that very kind of promise that a man of God like Micah takes into his heart and prays for its fulfillment—and God assures him that it will be so.

Micah Prophesies (7:16-17). Micah, not Yahweh, is again speaking in verses 16 and 17. (He speaks of *"the Lord our God"* and *"they shall be in fear of you."*) Micah prayed in verse 14. The Lord assured in verse 15. Now Micah describes what will be the result of God's faithfulness to shepherd His people.

To establish the promised blessing for His people, **the Lord will bring judgment to the world**. What He did with one land, Egypt, He will do with the entire world. The nations will be <u>powerless</u>—ashamed of what they thought was power (7:16a). They'll be <u>shocked</u> by what the Lord does (7:16b). They'll be <u>frustrated</u>—not wanting to hear the reports of what's happening, so they won't listen (7:16c). They'll be <u>humiliated</u>—licking dust like a serpent or like the crawling things (7:17a). They'll be <u>subjugated</u>—fearing the Lord and submitting to him (7:17b).

This is the Lord doing on a worldwide scale what He did when He delivered His people out of Egypt. As He separates the sheep from the goats, executing salvation and judgment, the world will witness something greater than the Exodus. The whole world will not be able to deny who the true God is and who His people are. What a day that will be!

So, who is a God like ours? He will shepherd His people, protecting and feeding them. He will judge their enemies throughout the whole world—shaming, shocking, frustrating, and subjugating them.

HE IS A GOD WHO PARDONS SINNERS (7:18-20).

In verse 18, Micah proclaims the uniqueness of the Lord. It's the most amazing aspect of our text—*Who is a God like you, pardoning iniquity and passing over transgression for the remnant of his inheritance?*

Micah's question causes us to ask another question. What has Israel done to deserve this? Hasn't Israel forfeited the promises? To say it another way, how do you explain the remnant? Why will there be a believing Israel? Because there's no one like God. Look what the Lord is doing for them.

He offers pardoning grace instead of deserved wrath (7:18a). He's *pardoning iniquity and passing over transgression for the remnant*—That's for the saved. From among *His inheritance* there will be a believing people of God, because of God's pardoning mercies. They deserve wrath, but He pardons them instead. What an amazing God!

He gives them steadfast love instead of everlasting anger (7:18b). They deserve *anger forever*, damnation. But *He delights in steadfast love*. He has loved them simply because He chose to do so, and He will faithfully love them even though they deserve everlasting anger.

He gives them conquering compassion instead of retributive justice (7:19). He treats their sins—and ours! —as an enemy. Sins <u>are</u> an enemy of God and of His people. People deserve wrath because of them. His power—*He will tread our iniquities underfoot*—becomes the instrument of His compassion. To show compassion for us, He had to overcome our sins. We now know that He's done this through the cross of His Son. At the cross, you see both God's power and God's compassion. He took His people's sins and trod them under His feet. He completely conquered them. Who is powerful enough to overcome guilt? Not us. Our Savior.

He offers complete reconciliation instead of partial access or probation (7:19b). *You will cast all our sins into the depths of the sea.* He heaves them away—all of them—to the unreachable bottom of the sea. He doesn't forgive half-way. If you're a Christian, rejoice that you are completely forgiven! Not only your past sins, but also all your future sins, are paid for in the Body of God's Son on that tree. God cast your sins away—not only removing the guilt, but transforming you. He's delivered you from the penalty for sin. He is delivering you from the power of sin. One day, He will deliver you from the presence of sin.

They find in God complete faithfulness, instead of being cast away by Him (7:20). *Faithfulness* speaks of reliability. You will prove yourself reliable to Jacob. *Steadfast love* is that famous word חֶסֶד (chesed), covenant faithfulness and love. "God, You will be faithful to us, *as you have sworn to our fathers from the days of old.*" Micah is confident that the Lord won't forget them. In light of that truth, he cannot help himself in verse 18 when he says, "*Who is a God like You?*"

Postscript

You may be a religious scholar, but have you ever seen God like that? Not just in your intellect, but with wonder in your heart? Has the Lord opened your heart to see who He is, so that now He's not just amazing factually; He's amazing to you? Do you see him as amazing in grace and mercy because He's shown grace and mercy to you?

"*Who is a God like You*, who would pardon my iniquity, who would pass over my transgressions, who would not be angry with me for forever, but instead show me steadfast love, who would have compassion on me and conquer all my iniquities, treading them under Your feet? Who would take all my sins and heave them as far away from me as the east is from the west…in fact, bury them in the depths of the sea! Who is faithful to me, reliable to me, steadfast in love to me? O Lord, who is like You?"

Do you know this God? If not, or if you're still not sure, look to Him today by looking to the One in whom He accomplished all of this. How did God do this? 2,000 years ago, God stepped out of heaven and came to earth, the second person of the Trinity. The eternal Son left heaven, took to Himself a sinless human nature, the God-Man. He lived a sinless life on this earth and died on the tree as a substitute for all those whom He would save. He died for all those who will place their faith in Him. He paid for all our sins in His own body, taking upon Himself the wrath of God that we might be set free.

Mankind has been given only one Savior. You know Jesus, or you don't know God. You come to Jesus, or you're still in your sins. You've read and studied Micah. Do you trust Micah's God? Be sure! Turn today from your sins and come to God's Son. He is the way. He is the truth. He is the life, now and forever. Will you come to Jesus today and be saved?

Oh, that millions more would open their mouths, give thanks, and exclaim, ***WHO IS A GOD LIKE YOU!***

Study Questions

Chapter 1 – God's Unlikely Means – 1:1-8

1. What was Micah's mission?
2. How would you describe your own mission? How is it the same as Micah's? How is it different?
3. Are you pursuing your mission? How? Why?
4. What do we know about Micah and his background?
5. What impresses (or doesn't impress) you when you consider a Christian leader? What should impress you?
6. What kind of kings did Micah serve under? Discuss the statement, "There is no level of wickedness so great that God cannot pour out salvation on my country or on yours."
7. Who served at the same time as Micah, and almost certainly knew him? How were they alike or different?
8. Do you know and treasure brothers or sisters in Christ who are radically different from you in their background?
9. What was Micah's main message? Is it relevant today? Why or why not?
10. What in this chapter do you want to remember and apply immediately?

Chapter 2 – Can You See God's Hand? – 1:2-16

1. How does the book of Micah's format serve to emphasize the book's main message?

2. In the courtroom scene, who is the main character? What roles does he have in the courtroom? Why is he qualified?
3. What words did this lesson use to describe some of the characteristics ("attributes" is the term theologians use) of God?
4. What two nations are the defendants? What city represents each of them?
5. What is Micah's attitude toward the message he's called to deliver?
6. What will the Lord do in judgment? Why?
7. Being barefoot and naked (1:8) pictures what for the people of Samaria and the northern kingdom?
8. Will Jerusalem and the southern kingdom escape? Why is the main focus on them?
9. What literary device or devices are used in 1:10-15? Review the list of towns and how the judgments fit them.
10. How do 1:10 and 1:15 both remind us of David?
11. What calamity is mentioned in 1:16?
12. What do you think the Lord's judgment will be concerning your own country? Why?
13. Do you need to repent?

Chapter 3 – Woe to the Oppressors – 2:1-5

1. What main sin is addressed in 2:1-2?
2. Those committing this sin are characterized in three primary ways. What are they?
3. What is covetousness? Do you ever use that word? If not, do you use a different term, or do you just not discuss the concept?
4. What six reasons did the chapter list as to why covetousness is a sin?
5. Would your friends and family describe you as covetous? How do you see yourself?
6. How is God's sentence on them symmetrical to (or appropriate to) their sin?
7. What do you think of their sentence?
8. Give examples of modern-day oppression.
9. Are there times when you and those around you are tempted to oppress people?
10. How can you resist being an oppressor? How can you help the oppressed?
11. Will proclaiming the gospel reduce oppression?

Chapter 4 – Religious Opposition – 2:6-11

1. What are three reasons why false prophets or false preachers might oppose someone who is proclaiming the Lord's truth?
2. What do they want Micah to do?
3. What do they say is wrong with the things Micah says?
4. The author says, "The most dangerous kind of preaching today is preaching that sounds right on the gospel, but distorts the effects of the gospel." What do you think he means by that?
5. What is a subtle perversion that's preached today? Why?
6. Micah's words are only disaster for whom?
7. His words wage war on whom?
8. What blessing from God will they miss, according to 2:10? Why don't they care?
9. What kind of preaching do the people want or deserve?
10. What kind of preaching do you seek—the truth, or something to make you feel good?
11. In all this gloom, where is hope? Who can offer hope?

Chapter 5 – Hope in Despair – 2:12-13

1. What in verse 12 tells us that there's hope?
2. What does the word "remnant" mean in this verse?
3. What does the Lord promise to do for the remnant of Israel?
4. Many prophecies have what two kinds of fulfillment?
5. Can you think of any other prophecy with multiple fulfillments? (You may want to look at Psalm 22 in reference to David and Jesus; Ezekiel 28:1-19 in reference to the king of Tyre and Satan.)
6. This prophecy points to what two periods of time?
7. In what four ways is the Deliverer pictured?
8. Which of these four ways seems most familiar to you? Which, if any, do you need to ponder more deeply?
9. What is your hope?
10. Why did God choose to work through ethnic Israel?
11. How can God use you in giving people hope in dark times?

Chapter 6 – Disastrous Leaders – 3:1-12

1. How can bad leaders be both a judgment from God and a reason for judgment?
2. What were Israel's leaders doing wrong, according to 3:1-3?
3. What would be the judgment for that?
4. What were the prophets doing wrong, and why?
5. Do you see any religious teachers today who are following their bad example?
6. What are some of the marks of Micah's godly leadership?
7. Does the definition of right and wrong matter? If you're a pastor or a church leader, how does this affect you?
8. How is the summary in 3:9-11 similar to—or different from—your nation's current situation?
9. What was the judgment to be for these sins?
10. How can this passage point us to Jesus?

Chapter 7 – Mankind's Only True Hope – 4:1-5

1. What is missing in man's heart?
2. What are two ways in which mankind's desires are perverted?
3. What time period is Micah describing here?
4. What five desires do we see in this passage? Who or what will bring about a world where these desires are fulfilled?
5. In what way or ways will the world be centered on God?
6. What will people want to get from the Lord in Jerusalem?
7. What will happen in the legal system? Would you be happy with such a legal system?
8. What will happen to military might?
9. What will people do that will indicate peaceful prosperity?
10. What resolution is listed, based on God's faithfulness? Is that your resolution?

Chapter 8 – How We Get There – 4:6-13

1. What will the Lord do to or for His people, according to 4:6-7?
2. What three roles does He fulfill in these verses?
3. What three results will His people experience?
4. How do these compare to the Lord's promises to Christians today?

5. Zion will be a safe place for the flock (:8), but before that, what kinds of judgment will the Lord bring (:9-10a)?
6. How will the Lord change things at last (:11-13)?
7. "Some people don't believe God has any plan for ethnic Israel. They don't see the signs." Are the Church and Israel identical? (You may want to read Romans 9-11, especially 11:26-29.)
8. In what ways do God's promises to Israel and to the church intertwine?

Chapter 9 – The Hope of Israel – 5:1-4

1. The first verse of Micah 5 points forward to which king?
2. What problem will Israel face in that day?
3. What will happen to the ruler?
4. What things are prophesied about the Messiah in verse 2? How was each of those fulfilled?
5. Have you pondered the significance of a prophecy concerning the village of Bethlehem (which had maybe 300 people) that was given about 700 years in advance?
6. Does national Israel today understand and acknowledge the meaning of verse 2? Do they have joy and peace (verse 4) in their Messiah's arrival?
7. Who is giving birth in verse 3?
8. What three things are noted that will happen in those days?
9. What do most of your neighbors or relatives or classmates or co-workers see as the best hope for solving this world's problems? In other words, what is their source of hope? What is yours?

Chapter 10 – Peace and Holiness – 5:5-15

1. Who is being delivered from whom?
2. Assyria is used to represent what?
3. There will be an abundance of what? When?
4. What are some of the ways that Israel will be blessed?
5. Israel will be changed. What four things will be taken away, according to 5:10-15?
6. How are all these things alike?
7. Have you had false hopes—false hopes that the Lord delivered you from?

8. According to your bank statement, your calendar, your plans and your daydreams, who or what are you hoping in right now?
9. Are there any false hopes that you need to abandon?

Chapter 11 – Tremendous Sin—Tender Indictment – 6:1-8

1. Describe the format of this passage.
2. Have you ever considered the thought of the earth itself witnessing?
3. What attributes of God do we see in 6:1-2?
4. What is His attitude toward his people in the first two verses?
5. If someone is weary of God, what does that say about God or about the person who's weary? Is serving God always easy?
6. What could cause such weariness?
7. What good things are mentioned that the Lord has done for his people?
8. What kinds of sacrifices does Micah mention in verses 6 and 7 as possibilities?
9. How do people attempt similar difficult but useless efforts today?
10. "The remedy for a sick spiritual condition is not greater external effort or multiplied activity." What does the Lord want instead? Why is this hard to do?
11. How can this encourage us? Is it too late for us to get right with God?

Chapter 12 – A Road Map for Repentance – 6:9-16

1. This chapter speaks of the danger when "sentiment replaces obedience." What does that mean? And what is the result?
2. What is repentance?
3. If we hear and fear the Lord, what will that look like in our lives? Passive, or active? Superficial, or deep?
4. What are "treasures of wickedness"? If you have some, what should you do about it?
5. In what ways are Christians tempted to use deceptive practices to gain money?
6. What would be the result of Israel's deceptive practices?
7. Can you think of any deceptions that you need to stop practicing?

8. Is there a minimum size before deceptions count? That is, what about "white lies?" Do they exist? Do they glorify God?
9. Are you walking in repentance?

Chapter 13 – The Heart of a Watchman – 7:1-7

1. Have you ever felt total grief at the situation around you? If so, when or why?
2. Can you hear the depth of Micah's grief?
3. What is the main cause for his grief?
4. What are signs that the foundations of the society Micah lives in are crumbling?
5. Do you see any of the foundations of your society crumbling?
6. The book referenced Matthew 10:32-40 and the rejection that can come because of our faith in Jesus. What specifics were mentioned?
7. How does Micah stay anchored?
8. What things will Micah do?
9. What does this say about his heart as a watchman?
10. In what ways are you a watchman?
11. How can you be both realistic and hopeful as a watchman?

Chapter 14 – How the Remnant Responds – 7:8-10

1. "When a nation—any nation at any time in history—has been presented the truth and then descends into great spiritual darkness, difficult times are ahead." Can you think of any examples of this— of nations where the gospel formerly had a strong presence?
2. Why would Israel's enemies want to rejoice over her? Do you see that same attitude today from enemies of God's people?
3. Verse 8 affirms what two facts that encourage the godly believers in Micah's day?
4. Are Israel's enemies the ultimate cause of her difficulties? Does the remnant know the cause?
5. Can Israel have hope in its future? Why or why not?
6. When was the last time you heard someone suggest that his or her nation's troubles may have been caused by the nation's sins? How was the message received?
7. Have you confessed your own part in your nation's sins?

8. When facing times of national disaster, what assurance do the people of God have concerning the future?
9. Based on what you know of the Lord's judgments and promises, what do you expect to see in the future in your own nation?
10. Re-read this brief passage. Are you able to make the words your own?

Chapter 15 – Who Is a God Like You? – 7:11-20

1. What is the connection between Micah's name and his question in verse 18?
2. "Has God's mercy toward you ever amazed you?" Discuss this—what are instances of his mercy that you are willing to share?
3. What day is anticipated in these verses?
4. What three statements about God did this chapter use to summarize these verses?
5. What does Micah ask the Lord to do for His people? What is the Lord's response?
6. How is the judgment of verses 16-17 even greater than the exodus from Egypt?
7. What is Micah praising the Lord for in the final verses of the book (verses 18-20)?
8. What words are used to describe the Lord's gracious actions?
9. What have you learned about God after going through this study of Micah? How has it affected you?
10. How and when can you share with others some of this truth about God?

www.ingramcontent.com/pod-product-compliance
Lightning Source LLC
Chambersburg PA
CBHW072028040426
42447CB00009B/1777